The Yellowknife Journal

WITH AN INTRODUCTION BY HARRY DUCKWORTH

TRANSLATED BY MARIE-THÉRÈSE HAUGHIAN AND KAREN HAUGHIAN

Book and cover design by Steven Rosenberg/Doowah Design.
Map design by Steven Rosenberg and Chris Molnar.

Printed and bound in Canada by Veilleux Impression à Demande Inc.

We acknowledge the support of The Canada Council for the Arts and the Manitoba Arts Council for our publishing program.

Canadian Cataloguing in Publication Data

Steinbruck, Jean
The Yellowknife journal

Includes facsimile reproduction of the 1802 journal, the French transcription and the English translation.
ISBN 0-921833-62-8

1. Steinbruck, Jean-Diaries. 2. Fur trade-Canada.
3. Northwest, Canadian-Description and travel.
4. Yellowknife Region (N.W.T.) -Description and travel.
5. North West Company-Biography. 6. Fur traders-Canada-Biography. 7. Manuscripts, Canadian (French)-Facsimiles.
I. Haughian, Marie-Thérèse, 1936- II. Haughian, Karen, 1957-
III. Title.

FC3212.3.S74 1999 971.9'301 C99-900283-X
F1060.7.S74 1999

Nuage Editions, P.O. Box 206, RPO Corydon
Winnipeg, Manitoba, R3M 3S7

It's with great pleasure that I introduce the reader to a remarkable artifact of the North West fur trade – a fur trader's journal, kept not on paper but on birchbark. For years there had been rumours that such a thing existed, and now here it is. The journal was kept during part of the winter of 1802–03 at a place called the Fort des Couteaux Jaunes, or the Yellow Knife fort – not, as one might first assume, near the site of the modern town of Yellowknife, but at a spot some fifty miles WNW of the village of Hay River, North West Territories. The author of the journal was John Steinbruck, an employee of the North West Company. We had heard of John Steinbruck before – he was one of those who accompanied the explorer Alexander Mackenzie on his first great voyage to the Arctic Ocean – but the birchbark journal is in his own hand and his own words. It is also a rare snapshot of the life endured by those who had to winter in unrelenting cold and darkness, on the edge of the sub-Arctic barrens of northern Canada.

For a European in the winter of 1802–3, a fur trading post on the Mackenzie River was the uttermost end of the world. A varied and adventuresome life had brought John Steinbruck to this place, and it is a pity that the only part of it that he recorded himself was this one winter trading season – the record that survives, written on birchbark, the subject of this book. Steinbruck's name marks him as a German. Practically the only German surnames to be found in the colony of Canada before the year 1800 belonged to the so-called Hessians, mercenary soldiers from Hesse and other parts of Protestant Germany who had fought for the British during the American War of Independence, and remained in Canada after the peace of 1783. John Steinbruck was one of these mercenaries.

According to the Hessian muster rolls, Heinrich or Christian Steinbruck (his full name was probably Johann Heinrich Christian Steinbruck) was born about January 1760 at Ermanstedt in Thuringia, and enlisted in a battalion of mercenaries that left Germany in April 1778, reaching Canada in September.

He served in Captain Hambach's company of Captain von Barner's battalion. The army heard of him last on July 19, 1783, when he deserted – the war had been over in all but name for more than a year, and Steinbruck must have seen opportunities in the New World that did not await him back in Germany. For the next six years his career is a blank, but evidently he worked in a French-speaking environment, for the birchbark journal is written in French, a language that he must have learned in the New World. During these silent years, Steinbruck found his way into the greatest business activity of early Canada, the fur trade.

For many generations the Canadian fur trade, based in Montreal but with important upper posts at Niagara, Detroit, and Michilimackinac, had been a good place for footloose and ambitious young men to spend a few years of their lives. Much of the trade in the French period was concentrated in the Mississippi valley, or around the Great Lakes – what was known as the *petit Nord*. But among the traders themselves, the most prestige was associated with the farthest places, the *grand Nord*, reached only after the longest canoe voyages. At first the *grand Nord* meant the Canadian prairies and the parkland fringing them, opened up by the explorer La Vérendrye and his sons during their search for that ever-receding rainbow's end, the Western Sea. And later it meant the northern forests stretching to the Arctic barren lands. Everyone knew that there was something special about the *grand Nord*, some special commitment when you went there. The new arrivals were welcomed by a mock-serious ceremony of baptism as they left the watershed of Lake Superior, the gateway to it.

The main produce of the Canada fur trade was beaver skins, of which between one and two hundred thousand were shipped to Europe from Canada every year, there to be used in the feltmaking industry in the making of hats. At the end of the twentieth century, when most people go bareheaded or else sport baseball caps, it's difficult to realize how important headgear was in the eighteenth century. Everyone wore a hat of some kind, usually of felt; of the felting materials, beaver wool was the best. Other furs were traded in North America as well, of course – otter, marten, lynx, wolf, fisher, wolverine, fox, mink, and so on – and these found their way from Montreal through London to Russia, and even across Siberia to China, there to adorn the mandarins and keep them warm.

In the years just after 1760, when Wolfe's army conquered Canada and converted a French colony to a British one, the fur trade hardly missed a beat. Young Canadians, who before the Conquest had worked as voyageurs or clerks for French entrepreneurs, readily found work with the new English-speaking employers who swarmed into Canada in the train of the army. Quickly the influx of new British capital drove the trade deeper into the north and west. By the outbreak of the American War of Independence in 1775, traders from Montreal had explored the upper Saskatchewan River, and had opened up the middle reaches of the Churchill. Three years later, in 1778, a Connecticut Yankee named Peter Pond, one of a number of loosely-connected traders on the Saskatchewan, took three canoe loads of goods beyond the upper Churchill, over a 12-mile trek called Portage la Loche, into the Clearwater River of the Athabasca basin. He wintered near the foot of the Athabasca River, just above where it falls into the Lake of the same name. His winter's trade there, with native customers who had never had a white trader on their home grounds, left Pond with more furs than his canoes could carry home.

This was a completely new province for the fur trade, this Athabasca. Beaver were plentiful, their pelts richly furred against the severe winter climate. The natives, members of the Dene nations who once had been obliged to send overland parties to Churchill Fort on Hudson Bay if they wished to trade, accepted the convenience of traders on their own hunting grounds. Eventually the fur trade's Athabasca country would extend all the way through the Mackenzie River watershed. Down the Athabasca River to Lake Athabasca they went; down Slave River to Great Slave Lake; up the Peace River to its headwaters in the Rocky Mountains; down the Mackenzie River itself; up the Liard to its headwaters in the southern Yukon Territory; up Great Bear River to Great Bear Lake; and on to the margins of the Arctic Ocean.

Peter Pond's Athabasca discoveries were not fully exploited at first. The War with America was on, and Canadian business underwent many difficulties. The high cost of trading in the *grand Nord*, with its long, long lines of transportation, had already driven traders into short-term coalitions. The most important of these was called the North West Company, whose origins can be traced to the early 1770s if not earlier. In the spring of 1784 a formally organized North West Company took charge of the *grand Nord*, under the direction of the brothers Benjamin and Joseph Frobisher, and their partner, a fast-rising entrepreneur named Simon McTavish. This new Company meant to control its costs by running the North West fur trade as a monopoly. High fur prices in Europe, during the years just after 1784, allowed the Company to entrench itself and make its partners rich. Rival Montreal traders, craving for a share of the grand Nord, did mount an opposition for a couple of years, but Simon McTavish bought out the most able opposition traders, and eased out, threatened, or ruined others. By 1788 a robust, consolidated North West Company was poised to exploit the full potential of Athabasca and the rest of its domain.

The North West Company was ruled from a depot on Lake Superior, where a cluster of substantial frame buildings stood at the eastern end of the Grand Portage, the nine-mile trek by which one began the journey into the *grand Nord*. Here, during a two-week period each July, those partners of the Company who had spent the trading season in the fur country – the "wintering partners" – made their rendezvous with the "agents", the merchants who represented the Company's interests at Montreal. These were lively, obstreperous meetings. Ingenious schemes, suspicions and resentments, nursed in isolation through long winter months, spilled onto the table and had to be sorted and shaped into plans for the next season. Somehow it was all done, and the wintering partners turned back into the fur country again. Outside the council hall, the fur produce of the old season was being transshipped into the large canoes for Montreal, and the trading goods for the new season were going across Grand Portage to be loaded into the smaller *canots du Nord*, heading for the wintering grounds. In the case of Athabasca, the voyage to Grand Portage was so long, and the travelling season so short, that the canoe

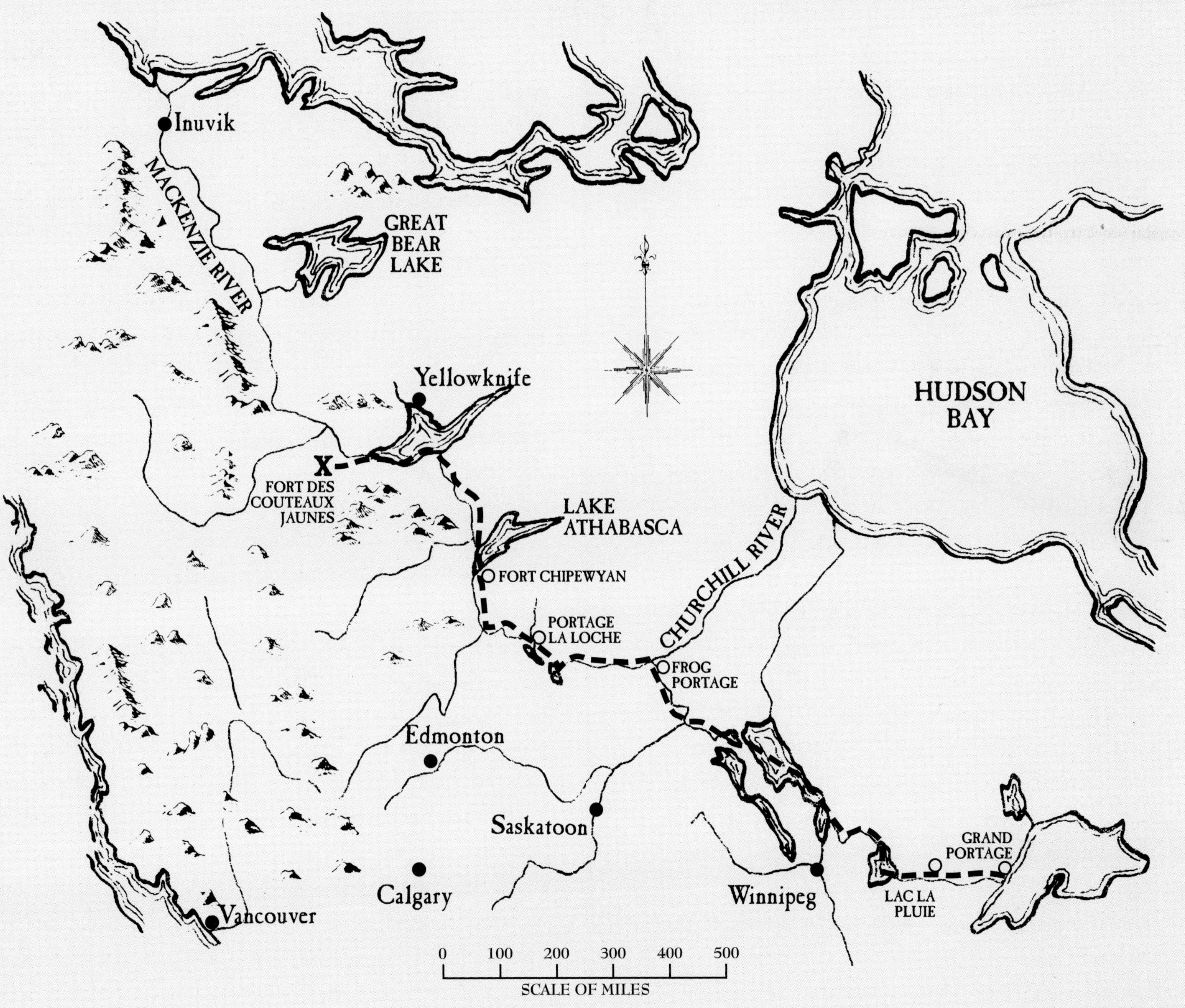
Inuvik
MACKENZIE RIVER
GREAT
BEAR
LAKE
Yellowknife
X
FORT DES
COUTEAUX
JAUNES
LAKE
ATHABASCA
FORT CHIPEWYAN
PORTAGE
LA LOCHE
CHURCHILL RIVER
FROG
PORTAGE
HUDSON
BAY
Edmonton
Saskatoon
Calgary
Vancouver
Winnipeg
LAC LA
PLUIE
GRAND
PORTAGE
0 100 200 300 400 500
SCALE OF MILES

brigades came only as far as a depot at Lac la Pluie (near the present Fort Frances). There the Athabasca men gave up their furs and received the next year's goods, thus saving four weeks of precious travelling time.

John Steinbruck entered the fur trade of the *grand Nord* at some point in the mid-1780s, during this critical period of expansion and consolidation. We do not know who hired him first, but it may be significant that he was among the trusted few whom the North West Company partner Alexander Mackenzie chose to accompany him on his first, celebrated voyage of exploration, down the Mackenzie to the Arctic Ocean, in 1789. Mackenzie had been a partner in the firm of Gregory and McLeod, one of the Montreal opposition companies that Simon McTavish had bought out two years before; Steinbruck, also, may have first worked for that company. In any case, the voyage on which the two embarked, with four voyageurs, in the summer of 1789 was an attempt to clarify the geography of Athabasca.

To the few mapmakers of the late 1780s who knew anything about Athabasca, the region was like a raft of geographical knowledge drifting vaguely within a wide patch of earth's surface, tethered to the rest of the charted world by a long, sinuous, canoe route. Peter Pond, the semi-literate genius who had discovered the fur trading potential of the region, and who spent several seasons in charge of it for the North West Company, had done his best to place Athabasca on the map. Lacking a means of determining an accurate longitude, Pond is believed to have resorted to dead-reckoning and the compass as his canoes made their way into the country, adding up his distances and bearings during the long sub-Arctic nights, doing the laborious trigonometry. From such a process Pond concluded that Athabasca was only a couple of hundred miles from the Pacific Ocean. His explorations had told him that there was a Grand River draining Great Slave Lake on the west. Now he guessed that this river continued westwards to the Ocean, where its mouth could be identified, he thought, as a deep bay, "Cook's River", that Captain Cook had discovered, but not plumbed, in 1778. If this speculation were true, the fur trade might supply Athabasca in future, not by the long canoe route from the St. Lawrence, but by a sea voyage from England and a short run up from salt water.

When Pond left Athabasca in 1788, another victim of the business intrigues of Simon McTavish, his successor, Alexander Mackenzie, was given the task of testing Pond's hypothesis by exploring the Grand River to its mouth. Mackenzie's famous summer canoe trip in 1789 showed that the Grand River – or the Mackenzie, as we now call it – actually drains not to the Pacific but to the Arctic Ocean. Conscious of the failure of his hypothesis, Mackenzie gave the name Disappointment to the river he had explored, and it was later usage that attached to that river Mackenzie's own name. His second overland journey, to the Pacific in 1793, further emphasized how isolated Athabasca was: between that country and the Pacific lay eight hundred miles in a direct line, perhaps fifteen hundred on foot and by water, and barrier after barrier of mountains.

John Steinbruck was on the first voyage of discovery, but not on the second. We do not hear of him again till 1798, when he is found on a surviving roster of the North West Company's partners, clerks, and interpreters in Athabasca. Probably he had remained in that country all along. The fact that Steinbruck is named at all on the 1798 roster shows that he was not simply a canoeman, for they were not listed there. His ability to read, write, and keep accounts would have made him useful as the keeper of a wintering post. But his status was irregular. A second surviving list, from 1799, gives his salary as 500 *livres*, using the old French money of account that had passed out of use in Canada with the coming of the British, but was still favoured in the fur trade. All the salaries in this list are in *livres*, but most of them are in multiples of twelve – that is, they had been negotiated in pounds Halifax, the currency which was now in use in Canada, at a rate of twelve *livres* to the pound. Almost the only salaries in the 1799 list that are not in even multiples of twelve *livres* were paid to men with French names – men outside the new economy of British Canada, in most cases men who would live the rest of their lives and would die in the North West. John Steinbruck, with his salary of 500

livres, was clearly of this second group. He was useful to the Company, but his prospects of advancement within it were dim. There were many young men, English-speaking but of Scottish birth, who entered the North West Company at this time for low apprentice's wages, but expecting soon to advance to proper clerkships, and eventually to become profit-sharing partners in the Company itself. There may have been a time when Steinbruck saw himself on the same career path, but in the Company one needed a patron – one of the partners, an uncle, cousin, or brother – to secure advancement. And it was easy for the partners' meetings at Grand Portage to forget those who toiled in the farthest corners of their fur trade empire.

The fragmentary records of the North West Company's efforts in Athabasca give us an occasional glimpse of John Steinbruck's activities. In the season of 1800–01 he seems to have been in charge of a small post at Lac la Martre, beyond the North Arm of Great Slave Lake. There is no information about him for the following season, but in the summer of 1802 he remained at the Great Slave Lake post, under the command of a young clerk, Ferdinand Willard Wentzel. Wentzel's journal for the period August 21 to October 15 1802 has survived, and it is helpful in understanding the context in which the birchbark journal was written. Wentzel refers to Steinbruck in a variety of ways – usually as "John," but sometimes "John Dutchman" and even "Monsieur l'Allemand." Practically no trading was done in summer, and the activities described in Wentzel's summer journal consisted of building or repairing the buildings and getting food.

They were also keeping track of a new fur trade opposition company that had made its appearance at Great Slave Lake only a season or two before. This was the XY Company (the name is said to have come from lettering on its packs). The Nor'Westers called them the Potties – said to be adopted from a *canadien* phrase signifying something of no importance, *une petite potée*. The activities of the XY Company were causing more and more consternation among the clerks and partners of the North West Company. By 1802, this new opposition had been in operation for about four years in different parts of the North West. Like the oppositions of the mid-1780s, this rival company was made up of Montreal traders who had not obtained a share in the North West Company's monopoly. But they were strengthened by an association with other traders who had formerly had a good living in the fur trade at Detroit, but now had lost that outlet with the handing over of Detroit to the Americans. The North West Company could do little to prevent its rivals from entering the nearer parts of the *grand Nord*, such as the Red and Assiniboine valleys, and the valley of the Saskatchewan, but they were determined to resist any entry into Athabasca. Few men in the fur trade were qualified to guide a canoe brigade over the long, tortuous canoe route to Athabasca, and for a year or two the North West Company kept the gate shut by the simple expedient of hiring all the men who knew the way. But in the spring of 1800 an intrepid XY Company clerk named Perronne got canoes from the North Saskatchewan, by way of Lac la Biche and Lesser Slave Lake, to the Athabasca River, and descended that rapid-filled stream to Fort Chipewyan. The wall had been breached, and Athabasca would be a scene of bitter rivalry thereafter.

By the summer of 1802, then, there was an XY Company post on Great Slave Lake, within easy view of the North West Company's post commanded by Wentzel. John Steinbruck and three voyageurs, named Adam, Tourcotte and Mandeville, were Wentzel's companions. A fourth voyageur, La Beccasse, arrived from Fort Chipewyan with letters from the partners on September 11; and another, Piché, joined the little community on the 24th. Some of the men would have had native wives and children, but as usual the journals pass over them in silence. Small native groups were continually coming and going, sometimes with meat to sell, but always with gossip about other natives, and stories of hunts, feuds, and intertribal warfare. Everyone was passing the time until the new outfit of goods should arrive from Fort Chipewyan, and the natives could get what they needed for the winter fur hunt. Steinbruck kept himself busy with such duties as plastering the outside of the chimney in the trading hall and building a hearth. He also was keeping an eye on the Potties, trailing them whenever a canoe was sent off, for fear they would encounter a native band with meat

or furs to trade before they reached the fort. The Potties' summer master was Perronne, the very man who had first achieved the penetration of Athabasca; his second-in-command was a teenager named Peter Warren Dease, son of a well-known Quebec family, doubtless brought along because he could write. Wentzel and his men had better knowledge of the country than the Potties did, and they were more successful in fishing and in buying moose flesh from the native hunters. Several of his journal entries make it clear that Wentzel was proud that he and his men were eating well, while the Potties were close to starving. At one point Perronne admitted to Wentzel that he was on the verge of abandoning the post completely because they could get so little to eat.

Plans were forming up for the winter's trade. The secret to taking the trade away from the Potties was to spread out to several posts, and keep the natives away from Great Slave Lake post itself. John Steinbruck would go to Lac la Martre, leaving as soon as the new trade outfit arrived. To the west of the Great Slave Lake post were two other posts, both maintained in the summer. The nearer of the two was the the Fort des Couteaux Jaunes (which Wentzel calls the Red Knife Fort) near the outlet of Great Slave Lake, in charge of an interpreter or clerk named Bostonnais. Further away was another fort, down the Mackenzie at the Forks of the Liard, in charge of a veteran interpreter named Laprise. Outfits would be sent to both places for the winter as soon as the goods arrived.

One matter that required attention was the care of an evidently influential native woman whom Wentzel called Madame La Brull. Madame La Brull was living at Great Slave Lake post for the summer, living on the fur traders' establishment, perhaps because her husband was away in one of the intertribal wars that were a constant feature of the summer seasons. Wentzel received instructions from his previous winter's boss, John Thomson, to take Madame La Brull to Fort des Couteaux Jaunes for the winter. When the plan was raised with her, she agreed at once, provided that she was given a few items of trade goods. Wentzel sent her off with La Beccasse, no doubt by canoe along the south shore of Great Slave Lake. La Beccasse brought instructions to Bostonnais to take good care of Madame La Brull. La Beccasse himself was to continue on to the Forks of the Liard, with orders that Laprise should get a new building up, in preparation for Wentzel's arrival to take charge there for the winter. It was all very straightforward.

Wentzel's feelings of superiority over the Potties evaporated abruptly on October 4. That afternoon, two canoes of the XY Company, with one clerk and eleven voyageurs and about sixty "pieces" of goods (each piece representing one of the 90-pound bales, kegs, or packages that the fur traders brought into the country), came down Slave River from Fort Chipewyan. The brigade was commanded by one of the XY partners, Alexander Mackenzie – not the explorer, whose northern travelling days were over, but a distant cousin whose imperious behaviour was to earn him the nickname "the Emperor." The North West Company's own brigade was nowhere in sight, and nothing more could be done to prepare for the winter until it arrived. Mackenzie and his clerk made no delay in inviting Wentzel and Steinbruck to a dish of tea, a little meat, and then something stronger. To his amazement, Wentzel was informed that the other Alexander Mackenzie, the explorer and long-time North West Company partner, had now joined the XY opposition. Mackenzie had been knighted by King George, the XY men proudly declared, and had earned a fortune through the publication of a book on his explorations. Wentzel was skeptical, confiding a few inconsistencies in the Potties' story to his journal, but it was alarming news. And it did turn out to be true.

More important for the moment, of course, Wentzel still had no trade goods to make up the winter outfits, and winter comes on fast and early on Great Slave Lake. On October 5, his journal notes, it was "snowing very hard & freezing still harder," and over the next few days the snow continued to fall. Soon there would be no chance of moving goods by canoe. The Potties were busy repairing their canoes, obviously about to set off for new posts with their wintering outfits. Wentzel asked John Steinbruck to prepare to go after them, wherever they went, and maintain an opposition alongside, but Steinbruck was unhappy about his equivocal

arrangements with the North West Company. Wentzel's journal records his complaints in French, and they may be translated as follows:

"I would have gone but you must tell Mr. Daniel Mackenzie when he arrives that I am not at all engaged; that he should give me 100 Louis for this year, for I was not listed in the roster of people this last summer. And what I did this summer was by my own free will. [And that I should have] an equipment like what the clerks of former times had by custom. You must tell him also that I am not being extravagant, and that I am not taking advantage of the times. That I ask only for the proper clerk's wages, and that if he wants to make an arrangement after that for several years it would be at the same [rate]. That I don't want to carry the name of clerk for nothing."

Wentzel told Steinbruck that he might remain at Great Slave Lake for the time being. Now the natives were coming into the post in earnest, and Wentzel, with nothing but fair words to give them, was trying his best to persuade them not to take credit from the Potties, but to wait the arrival of the North West Company goods. Wentzel's men were often at the Potties' post, where they were fed and made drunk. It was an atmosphere fraught with tension and wildness. Here are the last few entries from Wentzel's journal:

Tuesday 12th To day Adam & Piché went over to see the Potties – some time after they came back both a little in Liquor – att Dark X. Y. McKenzie Sent for them to go to supp with him – they asked my consent – I told them it would please me if they would remain Here – Not more than about 15 minutes after this – the Indians came to us telling us that the Potties Bourguois with his men was come to pillage us it was then quite Dark – I went out to beg of him not to pillage – found him in a Lodge close to the Hangard – he was attended by a great many men though I am ignorant of their names yet I shall write those I can with safety recollect, viz. Alex. McKenzie, their superior & leader, Edward Smith a Clerk, La Brie, one Cournoyé, one Daniel, & several others whom I cannot find their names after I had begged of him not to pillage us he jumped out of the Lodge with a drawn Sword in his hand & a Pistol in a Belt about his waist – striking the Lodge with his saying he would carry off – I said he should not upon which he took hold of the lodge & began to tare it off the Poles telling his men je vous montre un example – Piché called the Indians to our aid upon this McKenzie run after Piché & liked to have went after him with his sword Expossed when I drew my poignard & made him turn back – the dispute was put an end to through Smiths interference – Perronne came over but I did not see any arms about him – I told McKenzie the Shortest way would be to let the Indians settle himself as he thought which he agreed to – & then invited John & I with Piché, & Adam to take a walk over to supper with them when they first came over they were all a little in liquor— John & Piché got dead Drunk & La Brie got a quarreling with his Bourquois McKenzie – who in the quarrel drew his sword twice with an intention of running La Brie through the Body – Perronne & Smith were the only two of them that was not Drunk. Bad Weather –

Wednesday 13th. The little Lake entirely frozen over –

Thursday 14th. Adam went over to pay a visit to the Potties they recieved as well as usual – Monsieur Perronne asked him if he (Adam)

would be kind enough to get his poignard from the Indian as it had fallen out of its scabbard into the Lodge. – The poignard was found & brought to me I wanted to keep it but Adam & several of the men stood out that if I did not return it – that there would arise a great quarrel again – I was forced to acquise – I asked the Indian how he came by it – He told us that when the Potties was in hopes of getting him the night they came to pillage – He told them that he was afraid of N. West Fort they were fond of him – You are afraid Says X. Y. McKenzie there take that – giving him the poignard – Adam carried it over though much against my will – very bad weather"

It's a curious picture – Alexander McKenzie, the leader of the XY traders, himself drunk and violently out of control, and his subordinates reining him in and keeping the peace. As far as we know, the atmosphere of threats, bullying and defiance did not lead to any casualties at Great Slave Lake in this trading season, but McKenzie had chosen the methods he would use, and he would see the results.

When Wentzel brought this journal to an end on October 15, he had yet to hear anything of the North West Company's fall brigade. Only the force of his personality, it seemed, was keeping his little band of men together. He still did not know where the Potties, with their four canoes and their fresh outfit of trade goods, might set up posts for the winter, or what he might be able to do to compete with them.

The mystery of the late arrival of the North West Company goods is explained in another source – the journal kept by Peter Fidler, an alert and intelligent employee of the Hudson's Bay Company, who was doggedly maintaining a small post for his employers alongside Fort Chipewyan in this season. Alexander McKenzie, of the "New Company," Fidler recorded in his journal – this is the Potties' leader, the man they called the Emperor – had arrived at Fort Chipewyan with his goods on September 19 1802. Daniel McKenzie, who was to take charge at Great Slave Lake for the North West Company, arrived one day later. For some reason unexplained, Daniel let Alexander steal a considerable march on him: Alexander left Fort Chipewyan for Great Slave Lake on September 27, while Daniel did not set off for the same place till October 11. Alexander, as Wentzel records, arrived at Great Slave Lake on October 3, having made a brisk but not unusually fast voyage down Slave River. Once he did get his brigade moving again, Daniel was not so fortunate. Eventually news filtered back to Peter Fidler at Fort Chipewyan that the Athabasca winter had overtaken the North West Company brigade – they had been frozen in on the way down Slave River.

It is in this context, the problem caused by the failure of the North West Company trade goods to reach Great Slave Lake before freeze-up, that John Steinbruck's winter of 1802–03, recorded in the birchbark journal, is to be understood. The plans for the season, so carefully outlined by Wentzel in his summer journal, would have to be changed. Daniel Mackenzie would have left some of his men to guard the goods, partway down Slave River, probably arriving at Great Slave Lake post on snowshoes. A hasty council of war evidently decided to forget about sending John Steinbruck to the most distant post, at Lac la Martre, as originally planned. Instead, he would go to the Fort des Couteaux Jaunes at the western outlet of Great Slave Lake, close enough that a new outfit could be brought to him over the snow, once the season's goods had been sledded down the frozen Slave River. We do not know whether any attempt was made to set up a winter trade at the other western post, the Forks of the Liard. These decisions taken, John Steinbruck set off for his post. This is when the birchbark journal begins.

The birchbark journal is a typical example of a fur trade journal for the North West Company, a sort of official diary in which a record of the business of the post, the activities of the voyageurs and the native customers, and the weather, was systematically kept. The practice of journal keeping may have been modeled on the Hudson's Bay Company, where daily journals had been kept at each fur trade

post since the early years of the 18th century, if not before. Those journals, in turn, seem to have been modeled on ships' logs, whose purpose they shared – they ensured that the distant employers and investors in the trading enterprise received orderly accounts of how their property was being managed. What is in a particular fur trade journal depends on who was keeping it. Some are rich in detail and private thoughts, while others are the sparsest record of what was needed to satisfy the masters. John Steinbruck's birchbark journal is somewhere in the middle – generally businesslike as it records the all-important activities of trading furs and getting food, but with an occasional outburst of personal opinions, especially when he was feeling frustrated.

The largest holding of fur trade journals, by far, is in the Hudson's Bay Company Archives, now at the Provincial Archives of Manitoba in Winnipeg. Most of these journals are fair copies, sent from Rupert's Land to London for examination by the Governor and Committee of the Company, in their offices there. The North West Company seems to have been much less systematic in caring for the journals it required its employees to keep, and very few North West Company business records of any kind were retained by the Hudson's Bay Company after 1821, when the two Companies merged. Most North West Company journals that survive today were collected by one of the partners, Roderick McKenzie (1761?-1844), for a projected history of the Canadian fur trade that he never wrote. McKenzie's material passed to his grandson-in-law, Senator L. F. R. Masson (1833–1903), who published a very interesting selection of the journals in a two-volume work, entitled *Les Bourgeois de la Compagnie du Nord-Ouest*, still a standard source for Canadian fur trade history. After Masson's death the collection was dispersed. Some of the fur trade journals and other documents were sold, with the rest of Masson's library of Canadiana, at an auction in the spring of 1904, and most of those items ended up either in what is now the National Archives, in Ottawa, or at McGill University. Other items must have remained in private hands, and their present whereabouts are unknown.

A second group of North West Company journals survives as handwritten copies, among the transcripts known as the Selkirk Papers, at the National Archives of Canada. These papers have an interesting history. Thomas Douglas, Earl of Selkirk, had a long, complex struggle with the North West Company, featuring everything from court proceedings to cold-blooded murder, in the years just after he founded the Selkirk settlement at Red River. One episode in this struggle was Selkirk's capture of the North West Company 's depot at Fort William in 1816, during which he seized thousands of pages of North West Company papers, including everything from post journals, to lists of voyageurs, to private letters. All these papers were taken by Selkirk back to Scotland, and there they remained, at the Earl's residence at St. Mary's Isle, till Douglas Brymner, Canadian Archivist, sent young clerks to make copies of them in the period just before World War I. The house at St. Mary's Isle burnt down in the 1930s, and with it all the Selkirk Papers; but the copies made for the Canadian Archives preserve their contents. It is a story that illustrates the importance of copying and publishing original documents.

The birchbark journal seems to have a different history. This delicate object is in private hands still. It owes its preservation to the Mr. Henry de Lotbinière Harwood, and to his long-term interest in Canadian history and in preserving the cultural artifacts of this country. He obtained it from his father, Charles Auguste de Lotbinière Harwood, descendant of the Seigneurs of Vaudreuil, and son of one of the important circle of antiquarians and collectors that flourished in Montreal in the last century. The journal is remarkable in at least two ways – it is written on real birchbark, and it is in French. Hardly any of the surviving fur trade journals were kept in French, although French was the language of the vast majority of North West Company employees. Few of the Company's employees were literate, and most of those who were, the clerks and partners, wrote in English. Some anglophones could write a rudimentary but serviceable French, but did so only to communicate with francophone employees when necessary.

There have always been rumours that fur trade journals on birchbark existed, and so the appearance of John Steinbruck's example, in its way, is a sensation. Why Steinbruck should have used such a material is surely explained by the closing paragraph of Ferdinand Wentzel's Great Slave Lake journal for the late summer and fall of 1802, already referred to:

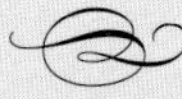

> I hope the Company will not censure me for want of attention if any thing should have slipped my memory having no Paper to keep a Journal In – but this I kept on the backs of old letters & other peices of Paper – I received but 1 quire to Keep a Journal, write letters, engagements & give tickets to upwards of 60 Indians last winter in the Grand River consequently I could have none remaining – therefore for the future [if the Company] expect a Journal they will Please give me Paper to Keep one.

Wentzel's journal, as we have it now, is a fair copy, which must have been made after the crisis was over. But this passage shows that there was no more paper at the Great Slave Lake post as of mid-October 1802, mere weeks before the start of the winter fur hunting season. Paper or not, Wentzel and Steinbruck would have to keep written records – not just their daily journals but, even more important, the daybooks showing what goods had been given on credit to the native hunters, and what furs had been received. The fur traders' birchbark canoes provided a solution to the dilemma. Each canoe was equipped with its own patching kit – pieces of birchbark, and lumps of gum to glue the bark over the rips and holes that were inevitable with use. Birchbark was a valuable material on Great Slave Lake, for the nearest canoe birch trees were two hundred miles away, on the Birch Mountains southwest of Lake Athabasca. But evidently the decision was made that Steinbruck, at least, should take leaves of the bark with him to keep his written records. Wentzel may well have done the same, though his winter journal for this season has not survived. This was probably not the first time that the bark was used for written records.

John Steinbruck's journal for 1802–03, then, consists of fourteen leaves of birchbark, varying somewhat in shape but each about four or five inches tall and nine or ten inches long. As the photographs show, the leaves were bound together along the left hand edge with string passing through five holes. Except for leaf no. 5 and the last leaf, there is writing on both sides. After some early adventures, which led to the cracking off of parts of the title page, the journal has evidently been well cared for, and almost no text has been lost, though much fading has taken place.

The birchbark journal begins with Steinbruck's departure from the North West Company's fort on Great Slave Lake, the Company's capital for the district, heading for his winter quarters of Fort des Couteaux Jaunes. The Slave Lake fort was originally established in the summer of 1786 under the instructions of Peter Pond, near the delta of Slave River. The post has continued till the present day, and now is represented by the village of Fort Resolution, but fur posts moved from time to time, and the exact site in 1802 is unknown. Steinbruck would have made his journey to Fort des Couteaux Jaunes on foot, probably on snowshoes, pulling a sled or toboggan with goods behind him, for the season was much too late for canoes, and much snow had fallen. He was accompanied by one Indian. Their route was along the south margin of Great Slave Lake, and the walk to the *Fort des Couteaux Jaunes,* very close to the entrance of Mackenzie River, was just over two hundred miles. This walk took Steinbruck and his companion six days, and the landmarks he mentions are mostly to be recognized on the modern map.

The Fort des Couteaux Jaunes was probably established in the season of 1801–02. The name is taken from the Yellowknife Indians whose main hunting grounds were north of the upper Mackenzie, and on the northwest side of Great Slave Lake. The Fort was on the south side of the river, at the very southern edge of the Yellowknife territory. According to Lloyd Keith, historian of the Mackenzie River

fur trade, it had been built to take advantage of the many beaver reported to be in the region southwest of Great Slave Lake. Manuscript maps of the 1820s show an "old Fort" or "Post abandoned" on the south side of the South Channel of Mackenzie River, opposite Big Island – this must have been the Fort des Couteaux Jaunes. The nearest modern community is the village of Kakisa, about ten miles inland. Hay River is about fifty miles SSE as the crow flies.

All along the margin of Great Slave Lake, as he made the march to his post, Steinbruck encountered Indians who were impatient to get their winter goods, so they could head inland to their hunting grounds. When they saw how few goods he had with him, several talked of going along the lakeshore to meet *"les Français avec les marchandises."* Little did anyone know how long it would take Daniel Mackenzie and his brigade to reach Great Slave Lake, let alone send goods to posts farther into the country. Since the canoeing season was over, any dispatches would be limited to what a couple of men could pull on sleds. Not till the evening of November 24 did Steinbruck get delivery of any further goods, when two voyageurs, Adam and Schmidt (or Smith, as other North West Company journalists call him) arrived from the main post, pulling the goods on sleds. Steinbruck instantly used most of the new parcel to outfit a number of Indians who had been waiting around the post, as the precious weeks of their winter hunt slipped away. More merchandise arrived on January 3, brought by Adam and a native companion, referred to as *le beau-frère d'Adam*, and thus probably the brother of Adam's native wife.

Although the purpose of Steinbruck's post was the fur trade, trading activities took up little of the time. The invariable pattern was that the hunters and their families would come to the post in the fall, perhaps bringing some meat, or furs that they had taken during the summer, but mainly to be outfitted for the winter hunt. Most of the goods they needed would be advanced on credit, to be paid for with the proceeds of their hunts in the late winter or spring. Once outfitted, the different native bands dispersed for their hunting grounds, and the fur traders would not expect to see them again until they had furs to trade. In the meantime, most of the post's activity as described in the journal was simply staying alive – cutting wood and getting food. Each loss of a hook or line, and every piece of damage to a net, is scrupulously recorded in the journal, for these were items on which survival depended, and the ironwork could not be replaced. Likewise, Steinbruck fretted about the constant danger of breaking his poorly tempered iron axe heads in the deep cold, for then he would have no means to cut his firewood.

Steinbruck's journal is full of references to food. There was some dried and "pounded" meat available at the post, highly concentrated but difficult to eat without grease. There were occasional gifts of fish from natives encamped nearby, while others brought in meat or fish which they sold for trade goods. The most dependable source was fish caught in nets or on lines, though even this source could not be depended upon, and more than once the traders went hungry. In the thinnest times they were not above eating wolverine, a dainty dish about whose merits the least said the better. For Steinbruck's post, the fishery (*la pêche*) was maintained up the river, i.e. probably in the South Channel, where the fish were attracted by the current. He reserves his greatest enthusiasm for New Year's Day, 1803, when, after three days with no food in the house except what had to be saved for an emergency journey in case the fort had to be abandoned, Steinbruck and the women feasted on four beaver tails. Normally the *Jour de l'An* at a fur trade post was the occasion for a real celebration, but nothing like that was possible till two weeks later, when a purchase of meat from the natives was followed by *une petite feste*.

Steinbruck's small group of voyageurs, Adam, La Beccasse, and Bostonnais, seem to have been capable men, although Adam, at least, made his own decisions and paid little attention to Steinbruck's orders. On January 7 the journal sarcastically refers to the fact that there were two masters in the house. Steinbruck was at a considerable disadvantage at this point, since his clothes were worn out and insufficient against the cold, a problem he remedied eventually by making himself a new coat from a trade blanket, and new trousers from some of the trade cloth. The other men were apparently more tractable, and in any case they spent much of their time away from the post. Steinbruck would not have

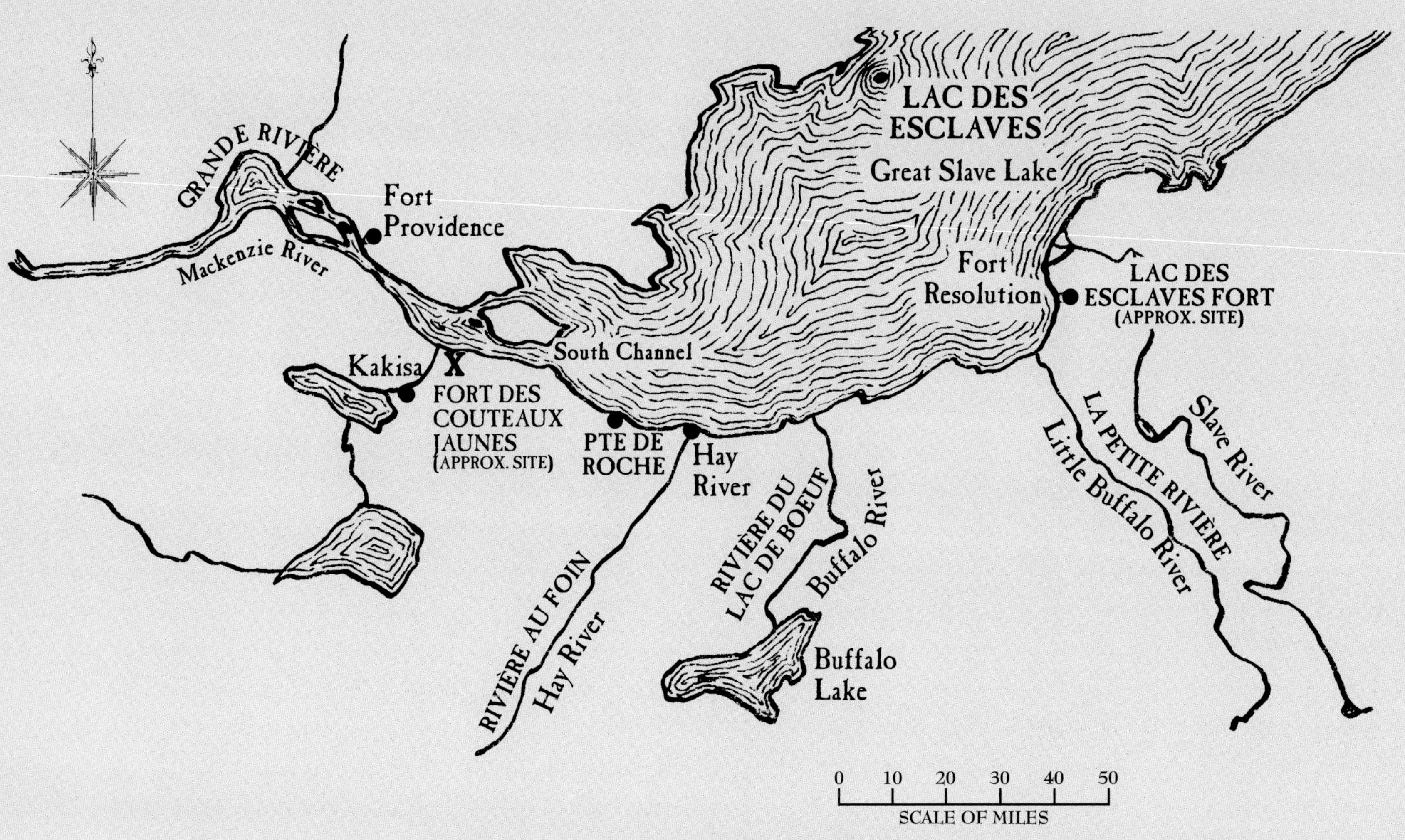

Names in ALL CAPITALS are contemporary with the birchbark journal. Other names are modern.

begrudged their absences, for that left the post with fewer mouths to feed – not just the men themselves, but also their native wives and children. Steinbruck mentions his own wife, *ma femme*, several times, and probably they had children – he refers once to "ma Familien," one of the few instances in which his misspelling of French betrays his German origin. In another place we read of leggings (*mitasses*) made for *la petite Fille*, likely Steinbruck's own daughter.

The natives with whom Steinbruck traded were Dene, and the name of the post itself suggests that they were of the Yellowknife tribe. If this is true, the post's customers were at the very southwest edge of the Yellowknives' probable range at this time. Most of this tribe was considered to hunt further north and east, even to the east of Great Slave Lake; but the positions of the tribes were in flux at this period, and there was constant warfare over hunting grounds. Few individual natives are named. A hunter called La Pouce Coupé appears twice, and there are references to the Chief of the Yellow Knives, an old man called La Babiche; and Adam's brother-in-law, whose name appears to have been Le Fou. We also encounter "Mr. Finlay's brother-in-law," whose sister must have been the wife of John Finlay, the North West Company partner in overall charge of Athabasca. The most intriguing figure is *Madame La Brull*, also called Madame Angélique in one place –apparently the wife of a leading Indian called Le Brull or Le Brûlé (the burnt one). Her importance for good relations with the hunters is indicated by the care that the traders took over her. She was waiting for her husband, who probably should have appeared in the fall. Steinbruck notes a bad dream that she had about her husband, which seems to have convinced her that her husband was not coming back. She then left the post to join her own brother for the rest of the season, but reappeared on January 22 with her *nouveau chefre*, her "new chief."

It is hard to determine how much fur was actually obtained for the North West Company at *Fort des Couteaux Jaunes*, through this marginal, if not perilous enterprise. All accounting in the Canadian fur trade was done in a unit called the *plus* – the same word was used in English and French – which was theoretically equal to the value of one prime beaver skin. The Hudson's Bay Company had a similar unit, the Made Beaver, which its field officers used to calculate their trade. The birchbark journal seems to record a total of 176 *plus* issued on credit, while 210 *plus* in credits were recovered, of which at least 38 were repaid in meat and other provisions rather than fur. A further 246 *plus* were "traded," that is, bought outright for goods on the spot, some 157 of which were in provisions. These figures add up to a total of 261 *plus* in furs, most of which would have been beaver. There were also three "packs" of furs, which may or may not mean the 80- to 90-pound packs, each containing about 70 beaver skins, which the traders packed for transport out of the country. Even these approximate figures are incomplete, as the birchbark journal does not take us as far as the end of the winter and spring trade. Nevertheless, it seems safe to say that the fur trade at Fort des Couteaux Jaunes yielded somewhere between five and ten of the fur trader's standard packs in 1802–03. This was of course an unfavourable season, given the delays in bringing the goods into the country; and the Mackenzie River was still at an early stage of exploitation. In 1807, Ferdinand Wentzel estimated that the whole of the River, from Great Slave Lake downwards, had an annual production of 65 packs.

On March 22, 1803, at midday, Ferdinand Wentzel, the senior North West Company clerk in the district, arrived from Great Slave Lake post, accompanied by one of his voyageurs, Turcotte. To Wentzel, according to his orders, Steinbruck surrendered the stock of goods and the furs, and brought the birchbark journal abruptly to an end. Why Wentzel took over the post in mid-season, we do not know for sure, but the insubordination of Adam would have cast doubt on Steinbruck's ability to lead.

There are no more journals for the Great Slave Lake and the Mackenzie valley until 1805, and till then the region lapses back into relative obscurity. The XY Company extended its enterprise farther and farther north and west, and the North West Company kept up with them. All over the Northwest, the rivalry between these two Companies was increasingly fierce, with frequent confrontations when clerks from both Companies tried to trade the same hunter's furs. The drunken behaviour of the XY Company's bourgeois at Great Slave Lake in the fall of 1802, shouting threats and waving his sword, had quickly set the tone in

Athabasca; elsewhere, there had already been more serious incidents. During the season of 1801–02, along the North Saskatchewan, a senior North West Company clerk, James King, described by a colleague as "in his prime and pride as the first among bullies," had tried to steal furs already traded by a young XY Company clerk, Lamothe. Physically outmatched but determined not to be humiliated, Lamothe shot James King dead. There were probably other murders, of which we have no record now – in later years, those who had lived through this period of bitter rivalry spoke of the details no more than necessary.

It is only through sources outside the Companies that we hear of one more episode involving John Steinbruck. Once again, that alert observer, the Hudson's Bay trader Peter Fidler on Lake Athabasca, is our first source. According to Fidler's journal, the trader known as "John Dutchman" was shot at Great Bear Lake in November 1804 by an XY clerk called McDonald. There are also some legal documents about the episode. One Étienne Gregoire, a voyageur from Lorimière in Quebec, was a witness to the incident, and made a deposition which still survives, but seems never to have been used in any prosecution. The killing had happened far in the Northwest, and it was easy to argue, as it would be again, that the jurisdiction of the Canadian courts did not reach so far. Gregoire's deposition may be translated from the French as follows:

"Montreal

"Etienne Gregoire voyageur, living at Lorimière, having taken oath deposes and says that in the autumn of the year 1804 he was engaged in the service of the North West Company at Lac d'ours [Great Bear Lake] in the Indian countries. That late in the fall of that same year a certain John Steinbrook, clerk for the said Company, with a certain Gagnier and the deponent, having seen two Indians of the Slave nation in company with John McDonald, clerk for Sir Alexander McKenzie & Co. [the XY Company] on the ice of that lake, who [paroissoit regarder] their fishing lines, the said Steinbrook with Gagnier and the deponent had advanced to speak to the Indians and learn where they came from. That having approached to about twenty paces of the Indians who were beside McDonald, the said McDonald told them to advance no farther, and showing his pistols that if they came closer he would shoot them with his pistol. That Steinbrook continuing to advance said to McDonald that he had no fear of him or his pistols, upon which the said McDonald fired at him his pistol loaded with a ball, and struck the said Steinbrook in his right arm and broke it. That at that time neither Steinbrook, Gagnier nor the deponent had any weapons, nor any intention of doing any harm to the said McDonald, and the deponent neither saw nor knew any reason at the time why the said McDonald should have shot at the said Steinbrook. That the said Steinbrook remained sick from that wound for three weeks, at the end of which time he died at Lac d'ours of that same wound, and the deponent truly believes that that pistol shot was the only cause of his death. And declares that he does not know how to write.

his mark

Etienne X Gregoire

Affirmed at Montreal the 13 September 1806.

J. P. Durocher [justice of the peace]

Shortly before John Steinbruck took to his deathbed at Great Bear Lake in the Arctic night, the agents of the North West Company and the XY Company at

Montreal were signing an agreement to amalgamate. A stout messenger was immediately dispatched on snowshoes to take the news to the nearest posts. Steinbruck was perhaps the last victim of the rivalry of the North West Company with the Potties, and his death actually occurred after the treaty ending the conflict had been signed. News of the amalgamation did not reach Athabasca till the spring of 1805, by way of Peace River, and at Great Slave Lake, the men would not have learned the news till high summer, at least seven months after Steinbruck's death. There may have been no punishment ever meted out to McDonald, the clerk who shot John Steinbruck. Peter Fidler names McDonald as one of the young bully boys whom the amalgamated Companies assigned to torment Fidler and his Hudson's Bay companions at Fort Chipewyan the following year.

A word about the printed text of the birchbark journal, and the translation. As can be seen from the photographs, many pages of the journal are quite legible, but others are faded, and in one place the birchbark has broken off, so that a few words are completely lost. Numerous attempts were made to render the faded pages more legible through ultraviolet and infrared scans, but the birchbark resisted modern technology, and ultimately, the traditional magnifying glass was the most effective tool for revealing the text. Understanding what is on each page, however, has been a challenge. French was not John Steinbruck's first language, and his spelling, though reasonably consistent, is all his own. He probably knew no French before he came to Canada, and then learned it phonetically, with little input from the written language. This would be why he usually writes *j'ai* as *jé*, for instance; while another of his favourite misspellings, *pardit* for *partit*, may have its origins in the Quebecois dialect. Steinbruck's French vocabulary is quite limited, so that translation is usually straightforward, though there are still a few obscure passages. There are also several fur trade words, each with a special, technical meaning. One of these, the unit of value called the *plus*, has been left untranslated for this reason.

Finally, it should be explained that the work of deciphering the text, and making the translation, has been entirely the work of Marie-Thérèse Haughian and Karen Haughian. They have sought advice and assistance from time to time, but the present lucid text is the result of countless hours of theirs, communing closely with the manuscript and digitized scans taken from it. Happily, the birchbark journal has been brought to public notice, after almost two centuries in obscurity.

For helping me to come to some understanding of the Canadian fur trade, and the world, remote in time and space, in which John Steinbruck lived, I have a few particular friends to thank. Lloyd Keith has shared with me his unrivalled knowledge of the Mackenzie River fur trade, for which I am very grateful. His forthcoming edition of the known North West Company journals for the Mackenzie district will bring that knowledge to a wide audience. Shirlee Ann Smith and Judith Beattie, successive Keepers of the Hudson's Bay Company Archives, gave me free access to the precious records in their care, besides words of advice and encouragement whenever needed. Warren Baker, unique repository of knowledge and enthusiasm for all aspects of the Canada fur trade and its personalities, gave me copies of key documents relating to John Steinbruck's death. I must also thank Jean-Pierre Wilhelmy for providing details of Steinbruck's origin and military career. There are many others whose contributions could also be acknowledged, and I apologize for not recognizing them here by name. I hope that they will find the birchbark journal as fascinating a document as I do.

Harry Duckworth

Journal

Pour le Fort des Coûteaux Jeaun

commencé le 6 de Decemb.r 1802

Par Jean Steinbruck

Pour N. W. Co.

[illegible] je Pardit avec une Sauvage Pour ale rentre
le Fort des Couteaux jaune en Soin la Beccass Thmet Coin font
Pardit en meme temps Pour [illegible] aun [illegible] tournet Son ma donnez
dise libre de bibre pour mon bagage nous avons pas faite grante chemi
car nous somme cacher longtemps Pour ner pas etre vue de la Potte
A la Beccass c'est amuse avec une orignal qui etois dans l'eau
Campez dans la Petite Riviere
7ieme Aujourd'hui j'ai encore perdit joli temps car je voyez la Potte su
le Lac Campez a la moitiez de la traverse
8ieme Cet Matin nous avons [illegible] Pardire [illegible] grand jour car il faisez une
Brume que l'on voyez pas [illegible] debent [illegible] Campez cet port [illegible] la Petite
9ieme Campez proche de la Riviere [illegible] Boeff
10ieme l'otre port de la Riviere je rencontrois 2 jenne Gences qui s'en allez au
Fort d'en pas je voulit [illegible] retournez avec moi
une pardie [illegible] [illegible] mais cetois inutile [illegible]
[illegible] Camp [illegible] [illegible]
me dit [illegible] [illegible] riviere [illegible] je trouve [illegible]
Cou[illegible]

6ieme Je pardit avece une sauvage pour alez prendre le Fort des Couteaux Jeaun en soin. La Becass Shmet & Coin sont pardit en meme temps pour pecher aux jes l'orignal. Lon m'a donnez dix livre de vivre pour mon voyage nous avons pas faite grante chemin car nous somme cacher logntemps pour nes pas etre vue de la Pottey et La Becass c'est amusez avece une orignal qui ettais dans l'eau Campez dans la Petite Riviere.

7ieme Aujourthui j'ai encore perdit di temp car je voyez la Pottey su le Lac campez a la modiez de la traverse.

8ieme Cet matin nous avons puis pardire q'au grand Jour car il faissez une Brume que l'on voyer pas quince pas devent soi. Campez cet port ci des la Pedite jes.

9ieme Campez proche de la riviere di Lac di Boeff.

10ieme Lotre port de la Riviere, je rencontrais 2 Jenne gences qui sen allez au Fort d'en pas. Je voulit les fais retournez avece moi……[page déchiré]/
une pardie d'amunition que j'avez mais c'etais inutile ca…. [page déchiré]/
chefre campez d'une pedite riviere d'ou je trouve la…. [page déchiré]/
me dit…. [page déchiré]/
Cou…. [page déchiré]/

6th I left with an Indian to take charge of the Yellow Knife Fort. La Becass Schmidt & Coin left at the same time to fish near the moose falls. I was given 10 pounds of provisions for my trip. we did not get far as we remained in hiding for a long time so as not to be seen by the Pottey and La Becass amused himself with a moose who was in the water. Camped by the little river.

7th Today I lost more time as I could see the Pottey on the lake camped in the middle of the crossing.

8th This morning we couldn't leave until broad daylight because there was a fog so thick that we could hardly see fifteen feet in front of us. Camped on this side of the little falls.

9th Camped near the river of Buffalo Lake.

10th On the other side of the river, I met 2 young men [braves] who were going to the Fort below. I wanted them to come back with me……[torn page]/
part of ammunition that I had but it was useless……[torn page]/
chief camped. In a little river where I find the……[torn page]/
told me……[torn page] /

4 Cette Matin les Sauteux qui etoit abbandonné a fort ty disant qu'il ettoit malade le Garcon de Peton a pris la place ettoit environ deux mois de partir leur ettoit bien traité dans sa loge fel loir le trouvez les Douce [illegible] que ettoit campez a la pointe de Roche et me dit qu'il allez [illegible] de Lac pour rencontrer les Francais avec la Marchandise et allez trouvez les Gence de la Riviere aux Foin campez [illegible] depuis leur [illegible]

[illegible] mes Peu [illegible] vers midi je trouvez toutes les Monde bien portant. Je trouvez une bon Eloge de Truite fait avec quoi je me fit faite une bon regalle qui quelle nettois pas faute pour moi

13 [illegible]

[illegible]

[illegible] plus [illegible] des [illegible]

[illegible] aux [illegible]

[illegible] de livres et [illegible]

[illegible]

16 Ce Matin on partit [illegible] Sauteux pour chaque a credit [illegible] ce que [illegible] ammunition gratis 3 mesure [illegible] en esperance d'abvoir une peu de [illegible]

11ieme Cette Matin les Sauvage qui ettais avece moi a restez disant quil ettais malade. Le garçon de Peton a pris la place. Je les donnez environ deux mesur de plomb car j'ettais bien traitez dans la Loche. Set Soir je trouvez la Pouce Coupe qui ettais campez a la pointe de Roche. il me dit quil allez Longue di Lac pour rencontrai les Francais avece La marchandus & allez trouvez les gence de la Riviere aux Foin campez une Pointe plus Loin.

12ieme Je mes Sui rendu au Fort apre midi. Je trouvez toutes les monde bien portant. Je trouvez une bon etoufez des Trouite fait avece quoi. Je mes sui faite un bon regalle quoi quelle nettais pas faite pour moi.

13ieme Aujourthui je pris compt de vivre. Je trouvez 410 livres de la viand Pillez 226 lb de graice 230 livre la viand en pieces. Aprez cela faite je traitez 3 train des Sauvages de quelles jettais contraint de paye 2 plus chaque & les prentre malgre eux encore.

14ieme Je envoye Bostonais & 3 jenne gence avece 80 livres des vivres et 60 lb pour les Sauvages. Je dandu un retz dans la Riviere.

15ieme Je visitez la retz et les trouvez cassez par la modiez a force de glass qui cetais amasse. Cet Soir est arivez 3 Sauvages pour chergé a credits

16ieme Cet Matin Sont partis. Je donné ce que javez encore damonition gradis, 3 mesur de Poudre 15 Balls & 10 Postes en esperance de avoir une peu de la viand fraiche.

11th This morning the Indian who was with me stayed saying he was sick. Peton's son took his place. I gave him approximately two measures of shot because I had traded a lot of loach. This evening I found Pouce Coupé (Cut Thumb) who was camped at the rocky point. He told me that he was going along the lake to meet the Frenchmen with the merchandise, and to find the men from Hay River who were camped on the next point.

12th I arrived at the Fort in the afternoon. I found everyone in good form. I found a good trout stew made with something. I had quite a feast even though it had not been made for me.

13th Today I took stock of the provisions. I found 410 pounds of pounded meat, 226 lbs of fat 236 pounds of meat in pieces. After I had done that I traded with 3 groups of Indians whom I was forced to pay 2 plus each and then take them back again against their will.

14th I sent Bostonais and 3 young men with 80 pounds of provisions and 60 pounds for the Indians. I set a net in the river.

15th I visited the net and found it broken in half from the force of the ice that had built up. This evening 3 Indians arrived to charge on credit.

16th This morning they left. I gave them the ammunition I still had free, 3 measures of powder, 15 balls & 10 buckshot in the hope of getting a little fresh meat.

Novemb 17 Cete Matin je fait Chaudiere de la viane car il n'y
a pas dautre chose Madam La Brull me Commande de aler
cherge de la graise molle pour mangé avec cete viand maigre

18 Cet Soir est aribez 2 jenne Gences de la Riviere aux Foin
pour boir si la Marchandies ettois aribez. je Commence a prentre la hache a la main Car les Bois que jai trouvez mes dure-
rez pas logntemps Le jenne Gence s'est mit pour attandre les Fran-

19 Cet Soir est aribez 2 bieullard di haute la riviere
qui mont donnez 2 Troutes

20 & 21 Pas de Noubelles 22 Cet Matin je enboye les
deux jenne Gence avec une demi rez a 6 Ligne pour boir si
jaurez quelque pieces de Poisson

23 aujourdhui lon a puis aller la premiere fois su la glace du
mois la Grand riviere est encore nette

24 Jettois en haute la ribiere pour boir si les jenne Gence
lont pris quelque chose je troubez un Troute que je porta
au Fort pour ma Familien

17ieme Cete Matin je fait chaudieur de la viand car il n y a pas dautre chose. Madam La Brull me comande de aler cherge de la graice molle pour mangé avece cete viand maigre.

18ieme Cet Soir est arivez 2 jenne gences de la Riviere au Foin pour voir Si la marchandus ettais arivez. Je Commence a prentre la hache a la main Car les Bois que j'ai trouvez mes durrez pas logntemps. Le jenne gence rest icit pour attantre les Francais.

19ieme Cet Soir est arivez 2 vieullard di haute la riviere qui mont donner 2 Trouites.

20 & 21 Pas de nouvelles.

22ieme Cet Matin jé envoye les deux jenne gence avece une demie retz & 6 Lign pour voir si j'aurez quelleque pieces de Poisson.

23ieme Aujourdhui lon a puis aller la premiere fois Sur la glass a Lac mais la grande riviere est encore nette.

24ieme J'ettais en haute la riviere pour voir si les jenne gence lont pris quelleque chose. Je trouvez un Trouite que je porte au Fort pour ma Familien.

17th This morning I made a kettle of meat because there is nothing else. Madam La Brull orders me to go and get some grease to eat with this lean meat.

18th This evening 2 young men from Hay River arrived to see if the merchandise had arrived. I have begun to use my hand axe because the wood I have found will not last long. The young men are staying here to wait for the Frenchmen.

19th This evening two old men from upriver arrived and gave me 2 trout.

20 & 21 No news.

22nd This morning I sent the two young men with half a net & 6 lines to see if I could get a few fish.

23rd Today for the first time we were able to go on the ice on the Lake but the river is still clear.

24th I went upriver to see if the young men had caught anything. I found one trout which I'm taking to the Fort for my family.

Cet soir Adam Shmit & une jenne homme sont arivez di Lac de Esclaves I mont aportez une peu de marchandises tel que cottons marc que excepte 2 prises di tabac donne toute huit di tabac a 5 saubages & une demie piez a Madame

25me aujourdhui je donnez 98 a credits a 14 hommes qui sont a la riviere au Foin et que jenboie par ces jenne Gencs qui sontsiet et 16 plus en tabac et munition gradius je arange encore 4 hommes qui sont dun autre port 25 plus a credits & 6 a gradius payez 23 plus pour B. tenai jenboyez la femme de Jos. Fournier que Bostonais a eu bien soin toute l'ette

26me ce jenne Gences sont partiez jenboye Shmit pour Conduir ceux de la Riviere au Foin & aprez Condinue sa route en bas de la riviere il y a encor 3 hommes ici que je arange pour chasse ici dans le bas de la grante Riviere

27me Adam a ettois en haute la riviere pour lebez la retz mais il a aportez en morceaux car elle ettois Gelé a la Glass

24ieme Cet Soir Adam Shmit & une jenne homme Sont arivez di Lac des Esclaves. Il mont livrez une peu de marchandus tel que c'ettais marcque excepte 2 press de Tabac donne toute Suit di Tabac a 5 Sauvages & une demie piez a Madame.

25ieme Aujourthui je donnez 98 a credits a 14 hommes qui Sont a la riviere aux Foin et que j'envoi par les jenne gence qui Sont icit et 16 plus en Tabac et munition gradus. Je arangé encore 4 hommes qui sont d'un autre part 25 plus a credits & 6 a gradis. Payez 23 plus pour B'tonais. J'envoyez la Femme de Jac Fourniez que Bostonais a eu bien Soin toute Letté.

26ieme Le jenne gences Sont pardit. J'envoyé Shmit pour Conduir ceux des la Riviere aux Foin & aprez condinue La route en pas de la riviere. Il y a encor 3 hommes icit que jé arange pour chassé icit dans le pas de la grante Riviere.

27ieme Adam a ettais en haute la riviere pour levez la retz mais il a aportez par morceaux car elle ettais gelé a la glass.

24th This evening Adam Shmit & a young man arrived from Slave Lake. They delivered a little merchandise which was as listed except for 2 arm-lengths of Tobacco. Gave some tobacco right away to 5 Indians and a half-foot to Madam.

25th Today I gave 98 on credits to 14 men who are at Hay River and which I send with the young men who are here and 16 plus in Tobacco and free ammunition. I again organized 4 men from elsewhere 25 plus on credit & 6 free. Paid 23 plus for Bostonais. I sent off Jac Fourniez's woman whom Bostonais took very good care of all summer.

26th The young men have left. I sent Shmit to guide those from Hay River and afterwards he is to continue the route downriver. There are still 3 men here that I have organized to go hunting here at the mouth of the big river.

27th Adam went upriver to raise the net but he brought it back in pieces because it was frozen in the ice.

Adam a Cassé la Grose hache. Tet tair Adam a declarez a La Femme
28 de La Brull que son Male est en has de la riviere. Je Servi de Demoin
et son a Compltez bien des Choses qui netois has initiule
Cet Nuit La Femme de La Brull at Mall revez de son Male Nous
29 Labon assurez que son reve pourez saccomplire. cest qui le fait
prentre enbie de partire pour trouvez son Frere. Je Lui donnez un bress
des Draps une Bress di Tabac 6 mesur des Poudre 50 Balls pour 2 plus de Bouche
10 lb de Viand Pillez. 6 des Graice 2 Colets de Caribou une demis plus en
Bil et Paiyez 2 plus pour elle pour une bine des Graice qui elle a pris
a Gredi et mangé abece ce parent
30 Est aribez 2 Taubages donnez 10 plus a credit pour des bibre et une piez di Tabac (gradin)
Gramspt fiere Les Taubages sont parctit Adam est aller abece eux pour
Charge 4 Placodes de Caribou Qui sont has Lain dicit.
2ieme Nous abons pousillez la Maison en detant Car son ne peut
2 resistez du Froit Nous abons tandes 6 Lign
pris une Frouite et une Loche. perdu un Lign et hamecon
3ieme Cete Nuit. La Femme des Bostonais est acouché dune enfant qui
4ieme a 6 orteille a chac piez sen machine d'homme devent et un autre de
Femme derieres en has des reins. et une Petite oreille desou les autre
pris une Frouite.

28ieme Adam a Casse la grose hache. Set Soir Adam a declarez a la Femme de La Brull que Son Male est en pas de la riviere. Je Serai de Demoin et l'on a complez bien des Choses qui netais pas initule.

29ieme Cet Nuit La Femme de La Brull a Mall revez de Son Male. Nous l'avon assurez que Son reve pouvez S'accomplire c'est qui le fait prentre en vu de partire pour trouvez Son Frere. Je la donnez un bress de Drap, une Bress di Tabac, 6 misur des Poudre, 50 Balls pour 2 plus de Poudre, 10 livres de viand Pillez, 6 des graice, 2 Colets de Caripoue, une demis plus en fil & Paiyez 2 plus pour elle pour une bine de graice qui elle a pris a Credit & mangé avece ce parent.

30ieme Est arivez 2 Sauvages donnez 16 plus a credit pour des vivre & une piez de Tabac gradis.

Decembre

1iere Les Sauvages sont pardit. Adam est aller avece eux pour cherge 4 placodes de caripoue qui Sont pas Loin dicit.

2ieme Nous avons bousillez la maison en detant car lon ne peut ressistez de Froit. Nous avons tandu 6 Lign.

3ieme Pris une Trouite & une Loche. Perdu un lign & hamecon.

4ieme Cete Nuit La Femme des Bostonais est acouché d'une enfant qui a 6 orteille a chac piez, un machine d'homme devent & un autre de Femme deriere en pas des reins & une petite oreille desou les autre. Pris une Trouite.

28th Adam broke the big axe. This evening Adam told La Brull's wife that her man is downriver. I can attest that we have accomplished many useful things.

29th Tonight La Brull's wife had a bad dream about her man. We assured her that her dream could certainly come to pass which made her decide to leave to find her brother. I gave her one arm-length of cloth, one arm-length of tobacco, 6 measures of powder, 50 balls of shot for 2 plus of powder, 10 lbs. of pounded meat, 6 of fat, 2 scrags of caribou half a plus in fishing line & paid her 2 plus for one bin of fat which she took on credit to eat with this relative.

30th 2 Indians arrived. Gave 16 plus on credit for provisions & one foot of tobacco free.

December

1st The Indians have left. Adam went with them to bring back 4 caribou haunches which are not far from here.

2nd We mudded the inside of the house because we can not bear the cold. We put out 6 lines.

3rd Caught one trout, one loach, lost one line & hook.

4th Tonight Bostonais' wife gave birth to an infant who has 6 toes on each foot, a man's machine in the front & another woman's in the back below the kidneys & one small ear beneath the other. Caught one trout.

5ème pris une troute & une Loche perdu une Lign & une hameçon
6e Nous avon tandu un rets pour avoir des apas
Nous avons visitez la retz mais rien pris di tout. Adam a pris
7e ide des harder et a pris pour son voyage 21 lo des libre une
grand Couteau & un Sac d'aurs il est arrivez un vieux qui est a la
Pêche par ici qui m'a apertez 2 troutes paiyé un plus. Jen ser
plus des Truet Car je point d'apas
8e il faut que je Cherge di bois [illegible] Car je rien une maubais
hache pour Casse les bois
9e Jetois voir la retz mais je riene pris
10e Cet Nuit la maison a pris a feuex par les Cheminez. Le vieux
m'a aportez une troute
11. rien de nouveaux. 12me Jetois levez la retz mais pas di poisson cet soir
est arrivez un sauvage qui m'a paiyez 8 plus en viand
12e fait 5 plus a Credits pour des libre Traitez une traine 2 plus que j'avez grande
besoin pour charier mon Bois car je le toujour charier a ...
13 & 14 pas de nouvelles. 15ème. Le vieux m'a aportez 2 troutes Le ...

5ieme Pris une Trouite & une Loche perdue une lign & une hamecon.

6ieme Nous avon tandu un retz pour avoir des apas.

7ieme Nous avons visitez la retz mais rien pris ditout. Adam a pris ide des pardir. il a pris pour Son voyage 21 lb des vivre une grand couteaux & un peau d'ours. Il est arivez un vieux qui est a la Peche pas Loin d'icit qui ma aportez 4 Trouites paiyé un plus. J'en prend plus de Truit Car j'ai point d'apas.

8ieme Il faut que je cherge du bois pouru. Car je rien une mauvais hache pour cassé les bois.

9ieme J'etais voir la retz mais je riene pris.

10ieme Cet Nuit la maison a pris a feux par les cheminez. Le vieux mes aportez une Trouite.

11ieme Rien de nouveaux.

12ieme Jetais lever la retz mais pas di poisson. Set Soir est arivez un Sauvage qui ma paiyez 8 plus en viand.

12ieme Fait 5 plus a credits pour des vivre. Traitez une treine 2 plus que j'avez grand besoin pour chariez mon Bois Car jé le toujour chariez a Lepa[ule.]

13 & 14 Pas de nouvelles.

15ieme Le vieux ma aportez 2 Trouites.

5th Caught one trout & one loach lost one line and one hook.

6th We have set out a net to catch some bait.

7th We visited the net but caught nothing at all. Adam decided to leave. For his trip he took 21 lbs of provisions a big knife & a bear skin. An old man who is fishing not far from here arrived and brought me 4 trout paid one plus. I am not catching trout any more because I have no more bait.

8th I must look for some dead wood because I have nothing but a bad axe to chop wood with.

9th I went to have a look at the net but had caught nothing.

10th Tonight the house caught on fire from the chimney. The old man brought me a trout.

11th Nothing new.

12th I went to take up the net but there were no fish. This evening an Indian arrived who paid me 8 plus in meat.

12th Did 5 plus of credit for provisions. Traded 2 plus for a sleigh which I very much needed to carry my wood because I have always carried it on my shoulder.

13 & 14 No news.

15th The old man brought me 2 trout.

16 [illegible] Outeou[illegible] — vider la Maison par de hors Car
[illegible] Dion et Perrac des Parapeua
17 [illegible] aujourdhui Car et [illegible] tout tracte hour
[illegible] de [illegible]ge
18 ce matin en arrivez [illegible] Gence [illegible]. [illegible] Cure de
Grace [illegible] sont restez [illegible] attentive les Francs
19 [illegible] en [illegible] qu'il sont deja ettoi,
[illegible] pour [illegible] les Francs [illegible] arrivez
20eme aujourdhui je redirez 26 [illegible] de Credits en comptant son Curtot &
[illegible] [illegible] queu [illegible] 3 plu
pour Pastonnes [illegible] je [illegible] ma portant des sache de embargez
le jeune Gence en haut de la riviere hour [illegible]
[illegible] pour [illegible] [illegible] pour [illegible] entre [illegible]
21eme les jeune Gence sont [illegible] lont [illegible]

16ieme Jettais Contraint des bousiller la maison par dehors car je ne peut pas ressistez le Froit dans cet barrac des paresseux.

17ieme Je ne pu pas sortire aujourdhui Car il faissez trop Froite pour mon Equipage.

18ieme Ce Matin est arivez 2 jenne gence Traitez 3 ou 4 livres de graisse de Castor. Il vont restez icite pour attandre Les Francais.

19ieme Set Soir est arivez 2 Sauvages qui lont deja ettais icite pour voir si lez Francais sont arivez.

20ieme aujourthui je redirez 26 plus a Credit en comptant Son Capots & manchés . Traitez 14 queu des Castor, une Castor. Payé 3 plus pour Bostonais. Je casse mon restant des hache. Je envoyez 2 jenne gence en haut de la riviere pour dantre le retz pour tager d'atrapez quellque apas pour dandre des lign.

21ieme Les jenne gence Sont arivez il ont aporter 2 inconnu &

16th I had to mud the outside of the house because I can't stand the cold in this barrack of lazybones.

17th I could not go out today because it was too cold for my equipment.

18th This morning 2 young men arrived. Traded 3 or 4 pounds of beaver fat. They are going to stay here to wait for the Frenchmen.

19th This evening 2 Indians who had already been here before arrived to see if the Frenchmen had arrived.

20th Today, I took back 26 plus in credits including his coat, provisions. Traded 14 beaver tails, one beaver. Paid 3 plus for Bostonais. I broke the last of my axes. I sent 2 young men upriver to set the net to try to catch some bait so we can put out the lines.

21st The young men have arrived. They brought back 2 unknown fish &

deux Truites et Cent [illegible]

22 [illegible] avec [illegible]

au [illegible] garçon

23 [illegible] une des femme Genev[illegible]

[illegible] plus [illegible] crédit [illegible] une truite [illegible]

24 [illegible] Cochon [illegible] hacher [illegible]

Prunes

25 [illegible] une Truite [illegible]

[illegible] Tabac [illegible] crédit [illegible]

26 [illegible]

27 [illegible] la Pointe [illegible] Lac des [illegible]

28 [illegible]

[illegible] ensuite [illegible] crédit

[illegible]

21ieme deux Trouite. il lont raportez le retz car le cortel a casser.

(contd)

22ieme Je dandu 7 lign avece des pointes de Bois Pourie car la jai nes que 3 hamecon.

23ieme Aujourthui une des jenne gences est pardit l'autre reste encore faite 8 plus a credit pris une Trouite & un brocheton.

24ieme pris 2 Loches Cassez 2 haches su les memme morcaue de Bois Pouris.

25ieme pris une Trouite il y a un Sauvage pardit lequelle aurer faite un Pacquette si jaure eu de quoi laranger.

26ieme pris un Brochton & une Loche.

27ieme Set Soir le Pouce Coupez est arivez di Lac des Esclaves donne di Tabac.

28ieme Aujourthui Traitez 2 plus 2 en viande 1 en San que Peausserie Jetais cherge toute cela en haute la Riviere fait 4 plus a credit. Pris 3 Trouites.

21st two trout. They brought back the net because the ground line is broken.

(contd)

22nd I put out 7 lines with barbs I made from rotten wood because I have only 3 hooks left.

23rd Today one of the young men left. The other is still here. Did 8 plus on credit. Caught one trout & one pike.

24th Caught 2 loaches broke 2 axes on the same piece of rotten wood.

25th Caught one trout. An Indian left for whom I would have made a pack if I'd had anything to make it with.

26th Caught one pike and one loach.

27th This evening Pouce Coupez (Cut Thumb) arrived from Slave Lake I gave him some tobacco.

28th Today I traded 2 plus, 2 in meat 1 in nothing but leathers. I went upriver to get it all. Did 4 plus on credit. Caught 3 trout.

[illegible] sont des nouvelles [illegible]

29 [illegible] il ne peut pas [illegible] de [illegible] de la bonne chère

Janv 1er [illegible] fait cette [illegible] pour deux an car depuis un [illegible]

1800 [illegible] que je [illegible] de [illegible]

des femmes [illegible] il faut que je les ménage en cas que je les

fille mais il faut [illegible] fort car si ma tache [illegible] je serez obli-

ligér [illegible] donc le [illegible] cependant je garde quatre queue de castor

traint malgré moi

que je mange avec les femmes. Cet hiver est arrivez dans

entre [illegible] le Chefre le couteau [illegible] pour charge de

ferettle [illegible] ce quatre homme qui sont a celle [illegible] armé [illegible]

[illegible] fait [illegible] par quelles mais je ne [illegible] une pipe de tabac

seulement pour les entraye

2 [illegible] Le Chefre me envoye huit queue de castor je la demande

[illegible] qu'ils demandez pour il a voit dit que quand il [illegible]

ne sort qu'il [illegible] toujour a manger aux traiteur sans [illegible]

29 30 31 Point des nouvelles. Je nest pas ete y faire rien a manger.

Janv 1iere 1803 Je ne peut pas fair de Louange de la bon chere que j'ai faite cette Jour de L'an. Car depuis un pout de temps je vue rien & sai quoi que je encore de la viand Pillez, mais il faut que je les menage en cas que je Soi obliger d'abandonez le Fort. Car si ma hache cass je Serez contraint malgre moi cepandant je garder quatre queu de castor que je mange avece les Femmes. Set Soir est arivez deux jenne gence di chefre du Couteaux Jeaun pour cherger des feraille Si ce quatre homme qui sont la ettais aranger il aurait faite Six pacquetes mais je ne pas une pipe de tabac Seulement pour les envoye.

2ieme Le chefre me envoyé huit queu de Castor. Je les demandez ce quil demandez pour. il a fait dir que quant il envoyez au Fort quil envoye toujour a mangé aux Traiteur Sens desein.

29 30 31 No news. I have not gone and made anything to eat.

Jan.1st 1803 I can not give enough praise for the good food I have made this New Year's Day. Because for some time I have seen nothing & know that although I still have some pounded meat, I must conserve it in case I have to abandon the Fort. Because if my axe breaks I will be forced to do so. Nevertheless, I have kept four beaver tails which I eat with the Women. This evening two young men sent by the Yellowknife chief came to get some hardware. If I had dealt with the four men already here too it would have made 6 packs but I have nothing but a pipe of tobacco to send with them.

2nd The chief sent me eight beaver tails. When I asked them what he wanted for them he had them tell me that when he sends them to the Fort he always sends along something to eat for the traders as a present.

Cet [illegible] [illegible] Toute [illegible]
des Carte [illegible] 1 [illegible] e [illegible] en [illegible]
un chese [illegible] je [illegible]
[illegible] me en [illegible] e [illegible] en present
premiere [illegible] [illegible] en [illegible]
qui a attendre [illegible] francais est arrete [illegible] n'etais 15 [illegible]
est arrivez [illegible] pour [illegible] croyant [illegible] apres midi
aurez de [illegible] fait [illegible] Adam [illegible] frere [illegible] qu'il y
arrive il ont laissez Bastonnais [illegible] a la Pointe
prendrez [illegible] jeune et y a quatre jour je recu une chemis
une petite [illegible] de [illegible] je ne parle pas
de ma [illegible] Guerique j'ai toujour [illegible]
dans [illegible] par [illegible] conscience [illegible] grand [illegible]
[illegible] Cet Marin [illegible] seulement le [illegible]
[illegible] filez [illegible]

3ieme Cet matin je faites 20 plus a credits. Traitez 2 plus en queu des Castor donnez 1 mesur de plomb & 2 piez gratis. Je envoyé aux chefre 8 mis de amonition point pour Son present quil mes envoyez mais a cause que je ne point envoyez la premiere fois que de Tabac. Le jenne hom qui a étais 15 jour icit a attandre aux Francais et pardit avece eux aprez Midi est arivez 2 Sauvages pour cherge a credit Croyant quil y aurez de quoi. Set Soir Adam & Son Beaux Frer &C. Sont arivez. Ils ont laissez Bostonais & La Becass a la Pointe Brulez, qui jeune il y a quatre Jour. Je recu une chemis, une boite de Coton & 5 feills de Pappiez. Je ne parle pas de ma Peche Car je prent rien. Quoi que jai toujour 8 Lign dans Leau par consicence la viand pilez Passe.

4ieme Cet Matin je envoyé au devant les hommes 10 livres de la viand pilez & queu de Castor.

3rd This morning I did 20 plus on credit. Traded 2 plus in beaver tails, gave one measure of shot & 2 feet free. I sent 8 measures of ammunition to the Chief, not for the present he sent me but because I had sent him nothing but tobacco the first time. The young man who was here for 15 days waiting for the Frenchmen has left with them. In the afternoon 2 Indians arrived looking for credit believing that there would be something. This evening Adam and his brother-in-law arrived. They left Bostonais & La Becass at Burnt Point (Pointe Brulez) who haven't eaten in 4 days. I received a shirt, a box of cotton & 5 sheets of paper. I don't mention my fishing because I catch nothing. Still, I always have 8 lines out because I am aware that the pounded meat is getting low.

4th This morning I sent 10 pounds of pounded meat & beaver tails ahead of the men.

5eme [illegible] arrivez [illegible] une [illegible]

qui nont pas ma[illegible]

car il [illegible] [illegible]

la Beccas [illegible] avec [illegible] [illegible] quelques [illegible]

rien [illegible]

tel [illegible] excepte [illegible] je recu la [illegible]

ia mais [illegible] rente que le longe [illegible] la prai[illegible]

ceux quil vit [illegible] mais [illegible] cela ne [illegible] par mon

compte

6eme [illegible] mais je envoyez un autre jeune homme au devan

la Beccas, car quant lautre trouve le chemin [illegible]

[illegible], il croyez quil sont toute passe avant retourn

e mes [illegible] ce qui est arrivez avec [illegible] nous avons

mange [illegible] car [illegible] ta[illegible] fait pas pour [illegible] une [illegible]

mais pour manger [illegible] [illegible]

5ieme Set Soir Bostonais est arivez avece une jenne hommes qui n'ont pas mangé depuis 4 jour que 2 Lign de chere car il lont point vue le jenne homme avec les vivres. La Becass a rester a la Pointe Brulez quoi quil n'ont rien pris depuis Adam les a laissez. Je recu le Butain tel qu'il etais mercqué exceptez 5 1/4 Bress des drap pour six, mais cela depente que j'elonge plus les bras que ceux quil ont Bressez, mais toute cela ne fait pas mon compte.

6ieme Cet Matin je envoyez un autre jeune homme au devent La Becass car quant l'autre trouve les chemin des Bostonais il croirez qu'il Sont toute passe & vas retournez. Je mes Suis pas trompez. Il est arivez aprez Midi. Nous avons mangé un carcachou Cet Soir pas pour fair une regale mais pour menage la viant Pillez.

5th This evening Bostonais arrived with a young man. They had eaten nothing in 4 days except 2 lines of food because they did not see the young man with the provisions. La Becass stayed at Burnt Point as they had taken nothing since Adam left them. I have received the Goods which are as marked except for 5 1/4 arm-lengths of cloth instead of six, but this is because I stretch my arms more than those who measured it, but none of it suits my needs.

6th This morning I sent another young man ahead of La Becass, because when the other one finds the trail of Bostonais he will think that they have all passed and he will return. I was right. He arrived after noon. We ate a wolverine tonight, not to have a feast but to conserve the pounded meat.

N.B. Si je maurez Partit il faut que vous donnez le commandemant a Adam & une raison pour quoi cela maurez pas fait des la pause de tout. Mais lon dit aux hommes je demande tous ecoutez Adam com moi memme. Je les parles pas de mon Peur car jé commandez Bostonais & La Becass & je croi qu'il n'y a pas grande gloire a Gagner & sil je etais aranger a la Prefs di Froit je lui donnerez bien les Fort tout ronde car je nes resterez pas icite car je voi bien que je sui desstinez Set hiver que pour avoir fair a chauffer les Femme { car Adam qui est commandant nest encor moins obliger de Pichez que moi qui sui sous lui & nous pouvons pas gardez les hommes pour les faire faim mais je suis si nul que je sui obliger des restez malgre moi.

N.B. If I were to leave the command would have to be given to Adam & one reason why this would not surprise me at all. But we say to the men: I ask you to listen to Adam the same as you listened to me. I don't talk about my fear because I command Bostonais & La Becass & I think there is not much glory to gain & if I was set up in a hurry for the cold I will give it my all because I will not stay here as I can well see that I am destined this winter to keep the women warm (as Adam who is commander is even less obliged to fish than me who is beneath him & we can not keep the men here and starve them but I am so low in the chain of command that I have to stay here even though I don't want to.

prim[e] cet matin [illegible] je ne sai pas [illegible] fait mais comme nous
som eteux maitre je dis nous avons envoyés les deux
et Adam en haute la riviere chercher [illegible] pour tout [illegible] il y a la
porpon cet jour la [illegible] c'est une bonne chose car il a
pris trois grose truite [illegible] manque la [illegible] que les autres
lon a trouver [illegible] d'erreur dans la [illegible] Tomin [illegible]
les Balls [illegible] de [illegible] le [illegible] de trois [illegible]
pour [illegible] une demi [illegible] de [illegible] qui n'etois pas necessaire
mais je fu bien surpris [illegible] qui [illegible] une seul article pour
moi meme car l'on sai bien que je su mal arrangé pour l'hiver
c'est pour [illegible] couvert [illegible] le donnai une au [illegible]
une que je donne a ma femme je fu contraint de prendre la
troixeme pour me fair un Capot car je n'etois pas encor arangé
en monde pour rester dans la Maison mes troupes controler pour
8 aujourd'hui les [illegible] sont partit nous avons envoyés Bostonnais
et la Beccasse [illegible] quelque Castor [illegible]
passés plus [illegible] Comme de la Beccasse d'une des jenne gens
[illegible] autrement de [illegible] fait [illegible] pour le bilan a credit
[illegible] un homme [illegible] grade

7ieme Cet Matin (je ne dit pas j'ai mais comme nous som deux maitre je dit) nous avons envoyer les Beaux Fr. d'Adam en haute la riviere avec 8 lign pour voir si il y a di poisson. Set Soir La Becass est arivez il a faite bone cher car il a pris trois grose Trouite & mangé les vivres ausi que l'on a avoyer. l'on a trouver d'ereur dans le peu de Putain que lon a recu 25 Balls 3/4 Bresses de Tabac de moin et 9 Postes de trop & 6 *norbes* pour 10 & une demie douze de Balafeux qui n'etais pas mercque. mais jes sui bien surpris de ne pas trouvez une Seule article pour moi meme. Car l'on sai bien que je sui mal arangé pour L'hiver. il est venu 3 couverts lon a ettais obligé de donnez une aux Sauvage une que je donne a ma Femme. Je Suis Contrainte des prendre la troixeme pour me faire un Capot. Car je ne süi pas encor aranger en monde pour rester dans La Maison. Me chaufez contre les feux.

8ieme Aujourthui les Sauvage sont pardit. Nous avons envoyez Bostonais et La Becass pour cherger 30 plus et quelque Castors en viand. Payez 3 plus aux compte de La Becass a une des jenne gences qui ettais au devant de lui. fait 11 plus pour de vivres a credit, donner 2 alleines & un demie piez di Tabac gradis.

7th This morning (as we are two masters, I do not say I but) we sent Adam's brother-in-law upriver with 8 lines to see if there are any fish. This evening La Becass arrived. He had eaten well because he had caught three big trout and also ate the provisions we sent him. In the pack of merchandise that we received we found in error 25 balls, 3/4 arm-length of tobacco less and 9 buckshot too many & 6 *norbes* for 10 & a half dozen bullets that were not listed. But I was surprised to discover that there was not a single thing for me, since they know I am ill equipped for winter. 3 blankets were sent. I was obliged to give one to the Indian, and I will give one to my wife. I had to keep the third one to make myself a coat because the house is not yet well arranged to stay in. I warm myself near the fire.

8th Today the Indians left. We have sent Bostonais and La Becass to get 30 plus and some beaver for meat. Paid 3 plus on credit for La Becass to one of the young men who went ahead of him. Did 11 plus for the provisions on credit, gave 2 fish hooks, and one half-foot of tobacco free.

Je pris de [illegible] drap pour me faire des Cullots
Car le mien sont pas de sortir Lun Bress de drap pour
ma femme & 4 Bresses di Labelle le jene home a aporte 2
petite Trouttes [illegible] hardet pour dantre deux demie
9me Mis L Adam [illegible]
retz en haut la riviere pris trois Trouttes aux Lezr
10me le retourne au Fort L Adam a reste
11 Adam est arribe mais a eu rien manze un & Carcachoux
12me par de [illegible] riviere
13me Adam a ettois en haute la Riviere bisider Levez
Pris un Poisson inconu
14me aujourdhuy Adam a Cassez les deux Bache qui
ont aporte dernierement Het Sois Bostonais &
La Gecass & un jenne homme sont aribe il ont aporte
30 [illegible] & 6 en viand & manze 2 en chemin donne un coup
de rhum aux homme & Taub[illegible]

8ieme Je pris di drap pour mes faire des Cullotes Car le mien Sont hors des Servis & un Bress di drap pour ma Femme & 4 Bresses di Tavelle le jene home a aportez 2 Petite Trouites.

9ieme Moi & Adam sont pardit pour dantre deux demie retz en haut la riviere. pris trois Trouites aux Lign.

10ieme Je retournez au Fort & Adam a restez.

11ieme Adam est arivez mais avece rien. Mangé une Carcachoux.

12ieme pas de Nouvelles.

13ieme Adam a ettais en haute la Riviere visider les retz. Pris un Poisson inconu.

14ieme Aujourthui Adam a Casser les deux haches quil ont aportez dernierement. Set Soir Bostonais & La Becass & un Jenne homme Sont arivez. il ont aporter 30 plus & 6 en viand & mangé 2 en chemin, donnez un Coup de romm aux homme & Sauvages

8th I took some cloth to make myself some pants because mine are no longer serviceable & one arm-length of cloth for my Wife & 4 arm-lengths of gartering. The young man brought 2 small trout.

9th Me & Adam left to set out our last two nets upriver. Caught three trout on the lines.

10th I returned to the Fort and Adam stayed.

11th Adam has returned but with nothing. Ate a wolverine.

12th No news.

13th Adam went upriver to check the net. Caught an unknown fish.

14th Today Adam broke the two axes that they had just brought. This evening Bostonais & La Becass & a young man arrived. They brought 30 plus & 6 in meat & ate 2 on the way, gave a drink of rum to the men and Indians.

1er. Comme nous abons fait maison [illegible] depuis [illegible]
et ces hommes lon jeuné meme et toute sont trouvez [illegible]
fort aux jour des lan nous abons fait une petite fête nous
abons donnez trois demiard de romme & nous abons pris la
ponce pour nous meme & Adam a fourni di[illegible] farine
pour fair une fricco

2eme. Cest Matin nous abons arranger les hommes pour [illegible]
Adam est partet abec eux pour les aidez donnez un [illegible] de
romm a leurs partance & une peux de la biand Bille [illegible]
Cet Soir est arivé une vieillard des quelle [illegible]
pl[illegible] di Credit traitez & plus en rozerion fait & plus [illegible] redure 10
donnez to poste un pied le Couteaux une alleine [illegible]

15ieme Comme nous avons fait mauvais chere depuis longtemps et les hommes Son jeune memme et toute Sont trouvez absent du Fort aux Jour des Lan nous avons fait une petite feste. nous avons donnez trois demiard di romme & nous avons fait la Ponce pour nous memme & Adam a Fournit di suger & Farine pour fair une Fricos.

16ieme Cet Matin nous avons aranger les hommes pour la Peche. Adam est pardit avece eux pour les aidez donnez un Coup de romm a leur partance & une peux de la viand Pillez & graice. Set Soir est arivez un vieullard des quelle je redirez 16 plus di Credits. Traitez 5 plus en rognion fait 5 plus a credits donnez 15 postes un pedite Couteaue une alleine & une pier gradis.

15th Because we have eaten poorly for a long time and the men are still young and everyone found themselves away from the Fort on New Year's Day we had a little feast. We gave three half-pints of rum & had a drink for ourselves & Adam supplied sugar & flour to make a feast.

16th This morning we got the men ready to go fishing. Adam went with them to help. Gave them a drink of rum when they left & a little pounded meat & grease. This evening an old man arrived from whom I took 16 plus of credit. Traded 5 plus in castoreum did 5 plus on credit, gave 15 buckshot a small knife a fishhook & a free flint.

[illegible] blan

[illegible] un brochet

[illegible] fort [illegible] boiste

[illegible] bonne [illegible] mange

[illegible] manon

[illegible] l'un et l'autre le matin

[illegible]

[illegible]

[illegible] heme saye

[illegible]

16ieme Les Sauvages est pardit pour aller en bas la riviere pour prende di Poisson & aller au Fort den bas nous pouvons pas pus les empechez. Adam a envoyez 2 petites Trouites.

18ieme Adam a aportez 2 Petite Trouites.

20ieme Jes Sui allez en haute des la riviere. Les hommes lont pris 3 Blanc & une morceaux aux retz & 2 Trouites au Lign.

21ieme Cete Matin pris un Blanc et un inconu au retz & un Brochet au Lign. Je me suis redournez au Fort avece une Trouite & les Brochet l'on peut voir Si nous font bonn chere a mange pour nous avece la Peche que lon faites. Car nous mangon que le Soir & avante nous partons lun ou lautre. le Matin nous prenont un coup des romm. Car je croi pas qu'il est nessecair que je marcque chaque Coup que nous prenont et ci nous vivons pas mieux comme a present les Sauvages Sen passonant di romm.

22ieme Set Soir Madam est arivez avece son nouveau chefre. Traitez 3 plus en la viand poudre & une peaux a parchemin. paiyé 3 plus pour les voir par les besoin que nous avons pour faire des

16th The Indians have left to go downriver to catch some fish and go down to the Fort. We couldn't stop them. Adam sent 2 small trout.

18th Adam brought 2 small trout.

20th I went upriver. The men had caught 3 whitefish and one piece in the net & 2 trout on the lines.

21st This morning I caught one whitefish and one unknown fish in the net & one pike on the lines. I returned to the Fort with one trout and the pike. We will see if we can make something good to eat with our fish. Because we eat only in the evening and before one or the other of us leaves, we have a drink of rum in the morning. I don't think it's necessary for me to record every drink we take, and if we don't live better than we are right now, the Indians will be crazed with rum.

22nd This evening Madam arrived with her new chief. Traded 3 plus in powdered meat & a little parchment. Paid 2 plus to have it because we need it to make

Cartes [illegible] pour des Zizes [illegible] racquetter sans cela elle [illegible]
donnez des quoi pour [illegible] mais [illegible] une petite [illegible]
tap [illegible] la petite fille
23me Ce Matin il sont partit donnez un piez di Tabac a chacun une
alleine d'un petite cantenaux a chacun de le Filles un bout de
Tabac a son Male 24me Adam est aller Couchez en haut
25 il est arrivez et portez 8 petites grosses truites
Adam est partit pour Couchez en haute la rivier
28me apres midi est arivez 2 Sauvages. je redonnez 26 plus di Credit le
29me [illegible] 1 les apreste car nous avons pas de Couverte a leur donner
cet Apres Adam est arrivez il a aportez 2 petites truites a 8 [illegible]
traitez 2 queue de Castor, un morceau de [illegible]
mis de Poudre 12 Pos [illegible] 2 pier a feux grades

22ieme Cordes pour fair des Lign & racquetes. Sens cela Madam nous donnez des quoi pour Soupez mais payez une petite pour des mittass pour la petite Fille.

23ieme Cet Matin il Sont pardit donnez un piez di Tabac a elle & une alleine & un petite couteaux a chacun des le Filles & un bout di Tabac a Son Male.

24ieme Adam est aller couchez en haut.

25ieme Il est arivez et portez 8 petite et groces Trouites.

28ieme Adam est pardit pour couchez en haute la riviere.

29ieme Aprez midi est arivez 2 Sauvages. Jé redirez 26 plus di Credits. les robbes il les aporte car nous avons pas de couvertes a leur donnez. Cet Soir Adam est arivez. Il a aportez 2 petites Trouites & 5 Loches. Traitez 2 queu de Castor & un morceau de la viand donnez un mis de poudre 12 Postes & 2 pier a feux gradis.

22nd Cords to make some lines & snowshoes. Besides that Madam gave us something for our supper but paid a little for leggings for the little girl.

23rd This morning they left. Gave one foot of tobacco to her & a hook & a small knife to each of the girls & a plug of tobacco to her man.

24th Adam has gone to sleep upriver.

25th He has arrived and brought 8 small and big trout.

28th Adam has gone to sleep upriver.

29th This afternoon 2 Indians arrived. I took back 26 plus of credit. They took the robes because we have no blankets to give them. This evening Adam arrived. He brought back 2 small trout & 5 loaches. Traded 2 beaver tails & a piece of meat, gave a measure of powder, 12 letters & 2 free flints.

20 Le [illegible]

[illegible] sur tout dieu par [illegible] [illegible] [illegible]

[illegible] Dieu [illegible] [illegible] arester [illegible]

[illegible] pecheur [illegible] [illegible]

[illegible] Contant [illegible] [illegible] [illegible]

[illegible] [illegible] [illegible] des Grans [illegible]

[illegible] [illegible] [illegible] Caster [illegible]

[illegible] petit [illegible]

[illegible] Adam est [illegible] en haute [illegible]

Adam [illegible] [illegible] [illegible]

[illegible] [illegible] [illegible] [illegible]

[illegible] [illegible] leur donner [illegible] homme

[illegible] [illegible] [illegible] [illegible] peché [illegible]

[illegible] peché [illegible] [illegible] [illegible]

[illegible] [illegible] [illegible]

[illegible] Adam [illegible] [illegible]

30ieme Les Sauvages Sont Partit pour pechez en haut pour amaser di Poisson et aler aux Fort d'en pas aprez. nous pouvons pas les areter avec rien. Cet Soir les Beau Fr. des Mr. Finlay est arivez. Set Soir nous avons manger des Loches que nos Pecheur a de la Foi & le rest qui bon a mangé & nous autre bien Contante de le trouvez pour ne pas Crevez des faim. Je faite la pottasse avec 6 livre de Graice.

31ieme Nous avons redirez 35 plus de Credits &Traitez un Castor donnez une alleine et un petite Couteaux gradis.

Fevriez

1iere Adam est aller en haute de la riviere.

2ieme Pas des Nouvelles.

3ieme Adam est arivez avece 3 Trouites acopagnez d'un Sauvages qui venait di Lac des Esclaves avece Villemur que Adam a laissez en haut car il ny a pas dequoi icit pour donnez une repas a un homme.

4ieme Adam est retournez en haut pour chergé La Becass qui est venu Set Soir.

5ieme Jé envoyez La Becass a la grand rivier & donnez 21 livres de vivre que lon etais en gache logntemps 2 mis d'amonition 2 pier a feux & une pair des Soulliez. Set Soir Adam est arivez avece rien.

30th The Indians have gone to fish upriver in order to stock up on fish and go to the Fort below afterwards. We could not stop them with anything. This evening Mr. Finlay's brother-in-law arrived. This evening we ate the loaches that our fishermen have at the moment and the rest of the food that is still edible and we were happy to have found it so that we don't starve to death. I made the stew with 6 pounds of grease.

31st We gave back 35 plus of credit. Traded one beaver, gave one hook and one small knife free.

February

1st Adam went upriver.

2nd No news.

3rd Adam arrived with 3 trout, accompanied by an Indian who was coming back from Slave Lake with Villemur whom Adam left upriver because there is not enough here to give a meal to any man.

4th Adam returned upriver to fetch La Becass who came back this evening.

5th I sent La Becass to the big river gave 21 pounds of provisions that we had in storage for a long time, 2 measures of ammunition, 2 flints, a pair of shoes. This evening Adam arrived with nothing.

[illegible] Mars

[illegible] mille [illegible]

[illegible]

[illegible] trop [illegible]

[illegible] compter [illegible]

[illegible]

[illegible] 2 gros [illegible]

[illegible] avec [illegible] particulier que [illegible]

[illegible] recommandez [illegible]

[illegible] attendre [illegible]

[illegible] enfant [illegible] son Beau frère [illegible]

[illegible] en pas [illegible] rejoin[illegible]

[illegible] arrivé a [illegible] est [illegible]

[illegible] a [illegible] en haste

[illegible] il est arrivé a [illegible] il a passé un horrible mauvais temps

6ieme Nous avons envoyez nos Femme en haute de la riviere pour quellque jour. Nous avons manger un carcachou qui navez que les os. Set Soir La Becass est arivez de ses voyage en dit quil a trop mal aux jambe pour marchez. Il a manger avece les autres de icit. Je nai pas pu le touchez.

7ieme Nous avons manger le dernier carcachoue. Je vous assur qui nettais pas bon.

8ieme Set soir les Femmes sont arriver d'en haut avec 5 Truite et un Brochet que lon a besoin. Les vieux nous envoye et Bostonnais a 2 gros Truite des rest aprez avoir bien de manger les Femme nous ont raportez que les vieullard qui etais la Sont pardit pour aller en bas. Quoique nous avons recommandez a Bostonais que quante il les voyez partir de venir nous averdir ou les odez leur Robbe, mais il les pas pus l'un ni láutre et voila Je peure quil Sont pardit. Que voulez vous que lón fass?

9ieme Adam est partir pour aller en haut pour envoyez son Beau Frer arrivez ce trois hommes pour les conduir en pas sil peut lez rejoindre donner 10 lbs. de vivre.

10ieme Cet soir Adam est arrivez avece rien. Villemur est pardit apres les Sauvages.

11ieme Rien a manger.

12ieme Adam est allez en haute.

13ieme Il est arrive avece rien.

14ieme Il a faite un horible mauvais temps.

6th We sent our women upriver for a few days. We ate a wolverine which was nothing but bones. This evening La Becass arrived from his travels. He said his legs were hurting too much for him to walk. He ate with the others here. I couldn't touch him.

7th We ate the last wolverine. I assure you it was not good.

8th This evening the women arrived from upriver with 5 trout and a pike that we need which the old men sent and Bostonais still has 2 big trout left after having eaten his fill. The women report that the old men who were there left for downriver. Even though we had recommended to Bostonais that when he saw them leaving he should come back and warn us or relieve them of the robes, he did neither and I am afraid they are gone. What could we do?

9th Adam left to go upriver to send off his brother-in-law. Three men arrived to lead them downriver if they can meet up with them. Gave 10 lbs. of provisions.

10th This evening Adam arrived with nothing. Villemur has left to follow the Indians.

11th Nothing to eat.

12th Adam has gone upriver.

13th He has arrived with nothing.

14th There was terrible bad weather.

[illegible] homme [illegible]

[illegible] bien [illegible]

Dans le morceaux [illegible] jetter [illegible] les [illegible] petites [illegible]

perte [illegible] dans la [illegible] [illegible] [illegible] Frente

Lhameçon [illegible] grand [illegible] [illegible] lhef

et les deux [illegible] porte [illegible] pres [illegible] bien [illegible] de fil

lautre cest en trois morceaux [illegible] Chaudieres pour

je cedez les tour des mon cuivre des Chaudieres pour

fair des ameçon car les autre sont presque toutes [illegible]

[illegible] [illegible] [illegible]

[illegible] [illegible] [illegible]

[illegible] fer [illegible]

[illegible] [illegible]

[illegible] pour [illegible]

[illegible] pour cete [illegible] des sauvages car cest [illegible]

[illegible] [illegible] Coup

[illegible] [illegible] de [illegible]

15ieme Jé ettais a la riviere pour tendre le retz. Les lign di jene homme pris 3 Loches et 3 moyenne Trouites.

16ieme Adam est partit pour pechez lui memme avece Son Beaux Frere.

17ieme Pas de Nouvelles.

18ieme J'ettais contrainte des Coupez une Petite Couverte pour faire des Nippes & mittene.

19ieme Dimanche. Le Beaux frere d'Adam a portez 4 Petite Trouites et les deux retz que une a restez la modiez Sou la Glass & lautre est par trois morceaux. Nous voila bien point des fil.

20ieme Jé odez les tour des mon Couvere des Chaudieur pour fair des amecon. Car les autre Sont presque toutes perdit.

22ieme Le Beaufrer d'Adam est arivez et amenez 9 Truites petites, 8 groce.

24ieme Est arivez deux Jenne Gences di chefre Couteaux Jeaun pour chergez de la merchandus principalement des Fusill.

25ieme J'ettais aux Lac cherge Adam pour voir ci il trouverez prope des allez voir cete Pande des Sauvages. Car c'est lui qui a toute Pouvoir des fair ce quil trouverez a son Coup et moi je suis un foll. Traitez 19 queu de Castor & un placodez d'orignal.

15th I went to the river to put out the net. The young men caught 3 loaches and 3 medium trout on their lines.

16th Adam has gone fishing himself with his brother-in-law.

17th No news.

18th I had to cut up a small blanket to make some winter caps and mitts.

19th Sunday. Adam's brother-in-law brought 4 small trout and the two nets, one of which stayed half in the ice and the other of which is in three pieces. We are now without any lines.

20th I removed the rim from the cover of my pail to make some hooks. Because the others are almost all lost.

21st Adam's brother-in-law arrived and brought 9 small & 8 large trout.

22nd Two young men arrived sent by the Yellow Knife chief to get some merchandise, primarily guns.

23rd I went to the lake to find Adam to see if he thought it was all right to visit this band of Indians because it is he who has the power to do what suits him and I am just a fool. Traded 19 beaver tails & one moose haunch.

[illegible] Adam est [illegible] avec les [illegible]
avec [illegible] tabac au chefe [illegible]
y sont [illegible] certain que ce [illegible]
cela [illegible] tabac de mes [illegible] que autre
a bien haché [illegible] fumer aux sauvages encore 3 [illegible]
[illegible] voila ce qu'il a pour [illegible]) [illegible] Petite
[illegible] 4 [illegible]) mais il ce promet de ne pas [illegible]
d'avantage [illegible] Moze [illegible] 2 petite [illegible]
[illegible]

27 [illegible] Adam a [illegible]
[illegible] il y a [illegible] avant
[illegible] il [illegible]
Mardi [illegible]
NB [illegible] avec Adam
et [illegible] d'avoir [illegible] de [illegible]
[illegible]
[illegible] deux [illegible]
2 [illegible]
[illegible]
[illegible] Adam [illegible]

Dimanche

26ieme Adam est pardit avece les Jenne Gence. Il a prit avece lui 2 1/2 piez di Tabac aux chefre 1 1/2 piez pour 10 hommes qui y Sont. J'en Sui certain que les Pout nes Sont pas lon que autre cela il a un Sac garni avec di Tabac de mes Jicque que lon a bien hachez pour fair Fumez aux Sauvages. encore 3 Grand & 3 petite couteaux & 7 pier a feux. Voila ce quil a pour cherge (J'espere pour le moin 4 Pacquetes) mais il ce promet des nes pas retournez d'avantage avece Si Peut des choses. donner 2 petites & 2 pier aux Jenne Gence gradis

27ieme J'ettais aux Lac cherger 8 Trouites depuis Adam a ettais change les retz et les Lign d'entroit. il y a bon peche apresent.

Mars

1iere Jettais aux Lac cherge 10 Trouites.

N.B. Bostonais est Malade. Sens cela l aurez ettais avec Adam et Son mal previent {je pence} d'avoir Pu trop de graice de boisson car il a la Coleche.

2ieme Il est arivez deux hommes de la riviere des Foin Pour voir si nous avons la marchandus. Il dise toute les autres pouvez aler en bas ci il y a rien Il mont faite present pour un plus de viande hachez. Voila qui vas bien. Adam pas icit et person coupable.

Sunday

26th Adam has left with the young men. He took with him 2 1/2 feet of tobacco for the chief, 1 1/2 feet for 10 men there. I am certain that the Pout are not far. This one has a decorated pouch of tobacco from my plug which we even cut finely for the Indians to smoke, as well as 3 large & 3 small knives, 7 flints. This is what he has to trade (I hope for at least 4 packs) but he promises that he will not return to take advantage with so few things. I gave the young men 2 small & 2 flints free.

27th I went to the lake to get 8 trout since Adam went to move the nets and the lines to another place. There is good fishing now.

March

1st I went to the lake to get 10 trout.

N.B. Bostonais is sick. Otherwise he would have gone with Adam and his sickness prevents him. (I think) he had too much to drink because he has the runs.

2nd Two men arrived from Hay River to see if we had any merchandise. They said all the others could go downriver if there is nothing. They gave me a present of 1 plus in meat. Everything is going well. Adam is not here and no one is responsible.

[illegible] sauvages [illegible] pour [illegible]
[illegible] Madame
[illegible] de tabac et [illegible]
[illegible] pour [illegible]
[illegible] pour [illegible]
[illegible] C'est [illegible] qu'il y a deux femmes [illegible]
[illegible] quand il faisait [illegible]
[illegible]
[illegible] il y a que [illegible]
[illegible]
lettres [illegible] beaucoup [illegible]
[illegible]
[illegible] est [illegible] avec [illegible]
[illegible] répondu [illegible]
[illegible] C'est [illegible] temps [illegible] ils ont [illegible]
[illegible]
[illegible] en grâce [illegible]
[illegible]

4ieme Les Sauvages Sont arangez pour pardir. Je donnez 3 couteaux 4 mis d'amonition gradis cet a dir un couteau a chacque homme et Madam Angelique a faite demander une envoyez un piez di Tabac et 1 1/2 piez coupez en quatre pour les vieullard. Je envoyez Bostonais tout malade quil est avece eux pour tagé des les doner Juscque Adam vien. Car ils mont dit quil y avez deux Jenne Gences tout pret de pardir quante ils sairont les Nouvelles dicit donnez a Bostonais 3 mis des Poudre 30 Castor & les rest des vivre quil y a icit et une bout de Carott Car il y a que un Bress de glace icite.

5ieme Jettais aux Lac visitez les retz avece La Becass et menne 8 Trouites & 3 Poisson Blanc aux Fort.

6ieme Adam est arivez avece son Beaux Frere qui ettais avece lui un autre Jenne homme et les vieux Babiche & un autre qui c'est garder au Lessendé Tu grand Lac. Car il faisse la mauvais temps quil ont perdit des vue il a traitez pour 4 plus de vivres 24 plus en graice 4 en viand pillez 10 en queu de castor 2 en Boisson 2 en viand & 3 plus quil depense en vivre pour Sen Venir et 50 plus en Peletrises. Il a donne 2 grande Couteau gratis. cet Petite Bande vien icit pour Sen aller en bas et vient pas de marchandus icite.

4th The Indians are ready to leave. I gave them 3 knives, 4 measures of ammunition free, that is to say, one knife for each man and Madame Angelique asked us to send one foot of tobacco and 1 1/2 feet cut in four pieces for the old men. I sent Bostonais, who is still sick, with them to give them this until Adam comes. Because they told me that there were two young men ready to leave when they heard the news from here. Gave Bostonais 3 measures of powder, 30 beavers and the rest of the provisions that were here and an end of tobacco twist because there is only an arm-length's thickness of ice left here.

5th I went to the lake to visit the net with La Becass and brought 8 trout & 3 whitefish to the Fort.

6th Adam has arrived with his brother-in-law who was with him, another young man and the old man Babiche. Another man stayed at the ascent of the big lake. Because it was storming they lost sight of him and I traded for 4 plus of provisions 24 plus in grease, 4 in pounded meat, 10 beaver tails, 2 in liquor, 2 in meat & 3 plus which they used on their way and 50 plus in pelts. He gave 2 big knives free. This small band is on its way downriver and does not want any merchandise here.

7 [illegible]
[illegible] dit [illegible] paroisse [illegible]
[illegible] Graton [illegible]
[illegible]
[illegible] homme [illegible]
[illegible]
[illegible]
[illegible] pour la [illegible]
[illegible]
9me Cet [illegible] [illegible]
[illegible] ont [illegible]
Adam [illegible]
10me [illegible]
[illegible]
[illegible]
une petite [illegible]
11me [illegible]
[illegible]
[illegible]
[illegible]

7ieme Aujourthui payer 37 plus en vivres que lon a recherchez & 12 pour Bostonais donner aux vieux La Babiche 1 couteaux, 1 Bal a feux 2 piere & une Bress des tavell gradis.

8ieme Adam est pardit pour la riviere aux Foins et Son Beaux Frere pour en pas de la riviere porter une Letre & une autre jenne homme pour retournez dans les Tere a laquelle payez 3 plus pour avoir mennez une Pacton de plus des autres Sauvages. donnez une petite couteaux une piere a feux & une alaine gradis. donnez pour 24 plus aux B.Fr d'Adam pour la Trouite quil nous a donnez. donner 23 lb de vivres 11 lbs. aux jenne homm et 12 que Adam a pris pour lui.

9ieme Cet soir est arivez trois jenne gences de la bande d'ou Adam a etais. il ont aportez 3 Pacton des plus pour les autres que Adam avez recu.

10ieme Je redirez 14 plus de Credits d'un jenne homme. Traitez 1 plus en viand. Payez 8 plus pour avoir menner les 3 Pactons des plus. donnez une petite Couteaux gradis.

11ieme Les Jenne Gence Sont Pardit exceptez Le B. F. d'Adam Le Fou qui ne vais pas retournez. Cet Soir est arivez six jenne gence de la riviere aux Foins avece des vivres et quellque plus. (Voila ce quil donne Pour je croi aux Sauvages d'arivez au Fort & pas de quoi pour alume la pipe.

7th Today I paid 37 plus in provisions which we went to get & 12 for Bostonais. Gave the old man La Babiche 1 knife, 1 bullet, 2 flints & one arm-length of gartering free.

8th Adam has left for Hay River and his brother-in-law left for downriver to bring a letter & another young man left for the field to whom I paid 2 plus for having brought back a pack of plus from the other Indians. Gave one small knife, one flint & one fish hook free. Gave 24 plus to Adam's brother-in-law for the trout he gave us, gave 23 pounds of provisions, 11 pounds to the young man and 12 which Adam took for himself.

9th This evening three young men arrived from the Indian band where Adam had been. They brought 3 packs of plus for the others which Adam had received.

10th I took back 14 plus of credit from one young man. Traded 1 plus in meat. Paid 8 plus for bringing back 3 packs of plus. Gave one small knife free.

11th The young men have left except Adam's brother-in-law Le Fou (Crazy One) who will not return. Tonight six young men arrived from Hay River with some provisions and a few plus. (This is what they give so I will believe the young men who come from the Fort & nothing to light the pipe.)

Je [illegible] 14 [illegible]

le Credit [illegible] donné à plus grand [illegible]

[illegible] Tisse 12 pieces pour Bostonais

[illegible] Les Beaux [illegible] parle [illegible]

[illegible] Beaux [illegible] coste de bois [illegible]

[illegible]

[illegible]

[illegible]

[illegible]

[illegible] de plus [illegible] la viande

[illegible] Dimanche [illegible]

[illegible]

[illegible]

[illegible]

[illegible] à plus [illegible]

12ieme Je traitez 30 plus en vivres 14 en viand & pillez retirez 16 plus di credit en vivres & 11 en viand et donnez 5 plus gradis. Set Soir La Becass est arivez avece une tournez de Boisson. Paye 12 plus pour Bostonais.

13ieme La Becass mes faite une age pour faire la Potage.

14ieme La Becass a Pichez une corte de Bois.

15ieme La Becass est aller au Lac avece le Fou pour refilez les retz et lign.

16ieme pas de Nouvelles.

17ieme La Becass est arivez avec 12 Boisson Blanc & 4 Trouites.

18ieme La Becass a Pichez une corte de Bois. Set Soir est arivez trois jeune gences avece di plus & de la viand.

19ieme Dimanches. Je recu 55 plus de Credits et 6 en vivre que je pris pour di credit en plus car jai rien pour Payer les plus aux jennes Gences. 20 plus qui rest sens etre payez. Traitez 4 plus en viand & la chefre a envoyer pour 3 plus de la viande pour avoir me fais de mancher a moi & donner 2 plus gradis.

12th Traded 30 plus in provisions 14 in meat & pounded meat & took back 16 plus of credit in provisions and 11 in meat and gave 5 plus free. This evening La Becass arrived with a round of drinks. Paid 12 plus for Bostonais.

13th La Becass made a pot-hanger for me to make soup.

14th La Becass chopped a cord of wood.

15th La Becass went to the Lake with Le Fou (Crazy One) to repair the net and line.

16th No news.

17th La Becass arrived with 12 whitefish, 4 trout.

18th La Becass chopped a cord of wood. This evening three young men arrived with some plus & some meat.

19th Sunday. I received 55 plus in credit and 6 in provisions which I took for credit in plus because I have nothing to pay the young men for their plus, 20 plus of which are still not paid. Traded 4 plus in meat & the chief sent 3 plus of meat for me to have something to eat myself & gave 2 plus free.

20ᵉ Le Beaux est aller sur Lac [illegible] les Saut, et Voir St Cir a Fourniez
di Lac des Esclaves avec quelque Marchandises.
21ᵉ Je arangez un Pacquete pour St Cir pour les envoyez demain
donnez une Brass di Tabac noir pour la Peche
22ᵉ Il est Partis. donnez 18 lb des bibre & 6 Queue de Castor & une
Coup de rom a trois hommes & une Piez di Tabac a St Cir j'envoye
Journez a la Peche. Environ Midi Mr Wentzel et Durcott
sont arivez di Lac des Esclaves & j'a fait revenir, St Cir donnez
un Coup de rom a Durcott & une Pacade d'orignal pour trois
23ᵉ je livrez les Buttain & Belatrix a Mr Wentzel suivent mes
l'ordre

20ieme La Becass est aller au Lac avece le Foux Set Soir St. Cir & Fourniez di Lac des Esclaves avece quellque marchandus.

21ieme Je aranger un pacquete pour St Cir pour les renvoyez demain donnez un Brass de Tabac noir pour la Peche.

22ieme il est pardit donnez 18 lb des vivre & 6 queuex de Castor & une coup de rom a trois hommes et une Piez di Tabac a St Cir. J'envoye Fourniez a la Peche auver Midi. Mr Wenzel et Durcott Sont arivez di Lac des Esclave. il a fair revenir St Cir donnez un coup de rom a Durcott & une Placodez d'orignal a eux trois.

23ieme Jé livrez les Buttain & Pelatrise a Mr Wenzel Suivent mes ordre.

20th La Becass has gone to the Lake with Le Foux (Crazy One). This evening St Cir and Fourniez arrived from Slave Lake with some merchandise.

21st I prepared a pack for St Cir to take back with them tomorrow. Gave one arm-length of black tobacco for their fishing.

22nd He has gone. Gave 18 lbs of provisions & 6 beaver tails & a drink of rum for three men and a foot of tobacco to St. Cir. I sent Fournier fishing around noon. Mr. Wenzel and Durcott arrived from Slave Lake and made St Cir come back. Gave a drink of rum to Durcott & a moose haunch to all three.

23rd I delivered my stock and pelts to Mr. Wenzel according to my orders.